THE ANGLO AMERICAN WORLD POWER

Taken Down From Within

The 'World's Greatest Scam'

Robert M. Wettergreen

Preface

It has been said that history has nowhere to go, the seas have been sailed, the mountains climbed...... with the world's economy 'stuck in the mud,' with ever increasing numbers joining the ranks of the 'educated unemployed,' especially the youth, while the world's refugee population continues to grow at an unprecedented rate.

This was alluded to in my first book 'In God We Trust' published in 2000. The first in a series of books that would follow America and the world on a 'roller coaster' run down to the Biblical Great Tribulation, Armageddon and for survivors a Millennium or 1000 years of peace.

The earth was created with positive intent. It was an unblemished rare beauty, a jewel in the cosmos teeming with life, with everything in abundance for mankind's enjoyment.

So what went wrong and how did the world arrive in its present woeful state? Hopefully this, a fifth book in the series will answer the question.

And yes, while it goes without saying that any mention of the Bible or a Creator in today's secular society, is an immediate conversation stopper, a 'turnoff' for many.....in what is now our totally deceived world. Is it not a great irony that despite the incredible advances made in science that show the actual truth about creation and intelligent design, that while most marvel at creation, little or no credit is given to a Creator, or the Creator, Almighty God?

As such I would urge you to go through the book with an open mind and decide for yourself whether or not the Biblical and historical evidence presented is relevant and truly lifesaving as is intended!

The prime focus of this book is on a prophecy found in the Bible Book of Daniel Chapter 2 *....(Most will know Daniel as the young Hebrew boy in the lion's den) But this prophecy shows much more, notably just how really close we are to the end of the world's present system, while providing a sure hope for the future.*

What was written over 2000 years ago is almost upon us, so if there is nothing else that you would take from this writing, my sincere hope is that you will not put the book down before you have read the following, it is so incredibly important as your entire eternity might depend on it;

Daniel revealed to Nebuchadnezzar, the King of Babylon the meaning of a dream featuring an immense image that would show the King the future not only of his Empire, but also the future of all the world empires that would succeed the Babylonian empire, right down to our day.

Notice how this comes across in Daniel 2; 28....there exists a God in the heavens who is a revealer of secrets that has made known to King Nebuchadnezzar **what is to occur in the 'final part of the days.'**

32. The head of the image was of gold, its breasts and arms silver, its belly and thighs copper, its legs iron, while its feet and toes were partly of iron and partly of molded clay.

Further Daniel told King Nebuchadnezzar that the image would be crushed and the chaff carried away by the wind with no trace of it being found. As for the stone that struck the image, it would become a large mountain and fill the earth, "

This would signify the beginning of God's Messianic Kingdom or Government here on earth – Daniel 2; 31- 35. The Kingdom we are taught to pray for in the Lord's Prayer.

So there it is, world history spelt out in a dream with the successive world powers represented by the image; the head of gold depicting Babylon, the arms and breast of silver was the Medo - Persian Empire. The copper belly and thighs was Alexander the Great's, Grecian Empire, while the legs of iron was the Roman Empire and the feet and toes of iron and partly molded clay would be today's Anglo-American world power.

Going further, notice in Daniel 2; 43.....whereas you beheld iron mixed with moist clay, they would become mixed with peoples of nations outside of God's people and would not prove to be sticking together. 44. And in the days of those kings, the God of Heaven will set up a kingdom that ..... will crush and put an end to all these kingdoms (including the world powers of today) and it, itself will stand to time indefinite.

Again, it is my sincere hope that you will properly appreciate that this is where we are in the stream of time and will be guided accordingly, for it is impossible for God to lie! Hebrews 6:18

And yes, while I do realize that what comes across might have some readers eyes 'spitting' blood...I would urge even these ones to persevere with an open mind, no matter how hard it may be, for with such knowledge there is great reward. Psalm

19 ; 11. I will try to ease you into the truth as painlessly as possible, but please fasten your seatbelts because the going, is going to get rough.

Perhaps the best way to make it more palatable would be to regard it simply as 21ˢᵗ Century.....'New Think' far removed the 'Dark Age' thinking that unfortunately still permeates and saturates the system through erroneous and fraudulent religious beliefs and thinking that lingers on.

Surely ,the recent advances made in science and technology in so many areas provide more than enough evidence to substantiate intelligent design and dispel archaic thinking such as random chance and evolution? Examples can be found in the human genome, DNA, nano technology, the human brain and the like. Hopefully people will finally 'get it' and see through all the Satanically inspired deception and 'dark age' thinking that has engulfed and plagued humanity since time memorial and mankind will move on to better times in harmony with the purposes of the Creator and his universe.

Notice something about creation in Romans 1; 25 ....those who exchanged the truth of God for the lie and venerated sacred service to the creation rather than to the One who created.

For it is written....Outside are the dogs and those who practice spiritism and the fornicators and the murderers and the idolaters and everyone liking and carrying on a lie. Revelation 22;15.

Content

WORLD WAR 1

Prior to 1914 the American people were mostly rural dwellers, farmers. The great Inter State highways that connect states and communities across America only came after the Second World War as did Radios, TV's, and other such modern era devices. Back then it was a different world with people looking forward to an age of enduring peace and prosperity.

America then was a proudly Protestant country, as too was South Africa, both countries having been built by people fleeing the persecutions the Church Inquisition in Europe. These countries had similar beginnings with Churches built in the center of towns, open air meetings held in public places and big family Bibles holding pride of place in homes.

People were clearly appreciative of their great God given blessings. Men folk would walk the streets in tailored suites with hats raised, in courtesy to show honor and respect to members of the opposite sex. Alcohol and tobacco were a no, no or at least held their proper place and were not openly on display as was gambling, debt and vices, not to mention corruption that in any form was not tolerated. Back then what are known as Judeo Christian principles and values held sway. But, the outbreak of the First World War in 1914 changed all that and came as a great shock to these folk who were generally well versed in Bible prophecy. It left many fearing and expecting the immediate fulfillment of Bible prophecy and the return of Christ, not realizing that 1914 would only be the start of the 'last days.'

Listening to a local Afrikaans radio station RSG in South Africa, I heard a Karoo farmer telling about a recent visit to the South African War Memorial at Delville Wood in France, where during the First World War where of the some 3,600 South African troops who entered the wood, only 400would march out!

A German General surveying the scene on horseback after the offensive, where only one tree was left standing was heard to remark.....*"Here lies the cream of South Africa's youth!'*

This came as a shock to me, in a sense it was a wakeup call upon the realization that a hundred years had past since 1914 and that we were now far into the Biblical 'last days'!

In fact ever since the beginning of the new century I had wondered how much more God needed to see before acting, with most prophecy having been fulfilled and with poverty, depression and the destruction of the earth rapidly reaching a point of no return.

The point of writing this is simply to have a quiet little heart to heart chat to help people understand and know exactly where we are in the stream of time and tell about something that every living soul urgently needs to know in what is now our totally deceived world.

Bottom-line what you are about to read is both historically and Scripturally correct and true beyond any shadow of doubt! What has been foretold will happen!

What are known as the 'Biblical *'time of the Gentiles*, ended in 1914 and with over 100 years having past since then, we are now far into what the Bible refers to as the 'Final part of the Days!'

1.   1914 A PIVOTAL YEAR IN PROPHECY

Now notice something else about the year 1914 foretold in Luke 21.24; ....*Jerusalem would be trampled on by the nations, until 'the appointed time of the (Gentile) nations' were fulfilled.*

Jerusalem had been the seat of ruler- ship of a long line of kings from the time of King David who had sat on 'God's throne ' in Jerusalem as the representatives of God himself; 1 Chronicles 29;23.

But that would soon change when in 607B.C. the capital of the Southern Kingdom of Israel, Jerusalem was overrun by Nebuchadnezzar and it's people taken captive to Babylon and God's temple destroyed.

According to the Bible this would mark the beginning of the Biblical 'Time of the Gentiles' that would continue 'seven' 'Biblical Times,'

Daniel Chapter 4.tells of a prophetic dream experienced by King Nebuchadnezzar of Babylon, that featured an immense tree that was chopped down with the stump banded with iron and copper and an angel declaring; *"Let seven times pass over it."* – Daniel 4; 10- 16. This would show how long God's ruler-ship would be interrupted.

According to the Biblical Day for a Year' principle the seven times would be calculated from 607 B.C as follows; 7 x 360 = 2,520 (Numbers 14.34 also Ezekiel 4; 6)......so by doing the math, the 'Time of the Gentiles' that began in 607 B.C., would end 2,520 years later in 1914.A.D. (less the zero year)

1914 would also mark the time when Jesus who had been sitting at his Father's right hand in heaven would be made King of God's Kingdom and for his heavenly ruler-ship to begin. Notice Psalm 110.1 ..."*Sit at my right hand until I place your enemies as a stool for your feet.*"

The Bible shows that Jesus has been ruling from heaven for over *100 years now. What would he have been doing? Notice Revelation 12 verse 7 .... War broke out in heaven; Michael (Jesus) and his angels battled with the dragon (Satan) and its angels 8. But it did not prevail, neither was a place found for them any longer in heaven. 9. So down the great dragon was hurled the one called devil and Satan who is misleading the entire inhabited earth and his angels were hurled down with him.10. Now has come the salvation and the power and the kingdom of our God and the authority of his Christ. 12 On this account be glad you heavens....Woe for the earth because the Devil has come down to you, having great anger, knowing he has a short period of time.*

1914 would also see the start of the First World War, fulfilling one of the signs given by Jesus in Matthew chapter 24. 3; ...*While he was sitting on the Mount of Olives, the disciples approached him privately saying "Tell us, when will these things be and what will be the sign of your (unseen) presence and the conclusion of this system of things?"*

Notice his answer in verse 7; '*Nation will rise against nation and kingdom against kingdom and there will be food shortages and earthquakes in one place after another. 8. All these things are a beginning of pangs of distress.*

Clearly, the First World War saw the start of a time of affliction that a century later has not yet abated. The Bible shows that Satan was the one who, in a sense, pulled the trigger. (1 John 5:1)

In 1918 before the troops had even left the trenches Spanish Flu invaded the battle field killing more American soldiers than did enemy fire. The flu quickly spread worldwide.

By 1923 the German currency was worthless and 1929 saw the beginning of the Great Depression.

And just 21 years after the end of the First World War in 1918, the world was back at war in 1939 with the start of World War ll.

The prophet Daniel also revealed to King Nebuchadnezzar that an immense image in the King's dream showed not only the future of the Babylonian Empire, but also of the world empires that would succeed the Babylonian empire, that would extend right down to our day.

Notice this in Daniel 2; 24 – 30. The image's head was of gold, its breasts and arms were of silver, its belly and thighs were of copper, its legs were of iron while its feet and toes were partly of iron and partly of molded clay.

Further Daniel told King Nebuchadnezzar that the image would be crushed and the chaff carried away by the wind with no trace of it being found. As for the stone that struck the image, it would become a large mountain and fill the earth,"

This would be the beginning of God's Messianic Kingdom or Government here on earth – Daniel 2; 31- 35.

So there it is, world history spelt out in a dream with the successive world powers represented by this image; The head of gold being Babylon, the arms and breast of silver representing the Medo - Persian Empire. The copper belly and thighs being Alexander the Great's, Grecian Empire, with the legs of iron depicting the Roman Empire, while the feet and toes of iron and partly clay would be today's Anglo-American world power.

Notice Daniel 2; 43.....*whereas you beheld iron mixed with most clay, they will not prove to be sticking together. 44. And in the days of those kings or (powers) the God of Heaven will set up a kingdom that ..... crush and put an end to all these kingdoms and itself will stand to time indefinite.*

So, according to the Holy Scriptures that is how God's Kingdom will come to be established here on the earth in our very day! That is the reality of the situation that it would seem, few are aware of....

With this now being so very close, the big question for everyone to seriously consider is.....whether your name will be found *written in the book of life Revelation 13.8?*

About this time, notice further in Daniel 12. 1 At this time....*Michael (Jesus) will stand up...and* **there will certainly occur a time of distress (The Biblical Great Tribulation)***such as not occurred since there came to be a nation. And during that time your people will escape; every one found written down in the book (of life.).4. As for you, O Daniel seal up the book until the time of the end. Many will rove around and true knowledge will become abundant. 10. Many will cleanse themselves and be refined. And certainly* *the wicked will act wickedly and no wicked ones will understand. But the ones having insight will understand.*

For just over an entire century since 1914, the *'four horsemen of the apocalypse'* have been at a full gallop with few people seeming to know or even seeming to care, so great is the Satanic deception.

What most people don't know and urgently need to know is that this it, we are now standing at the end of time, with very few prophesy's yet to be fulfilled.

So, why the deafening silence from the clergy, the mainline Churches of Christendom, the media, our leaders? How could such vital truth from the Bible have been missed?

Might the answer be that the 'wicked one' the world's present unseen ruler Satan the Devil knows that his time is up and doesn't care what you believe just as long as it is not the truth and wants to take an unsuspecting humanity down with him to leave God with an 'empty victory', so great is the hatred.

He hates! He hates God, Jesus, even his own Demons and certainly all of God's children, the human family!

The reason being that;...If he cannot have all the glory, nobody will, that is the mindset! Likely he believes that he can still win by having everyone marked with what in Scripture is referred to as the 'mark of the beast' ...something that will be discussed in the Chapter that deals with Revelation Chapter 13.

What is coming will affect every living soul, surely that is reason enough for everyone to start taking notice of what is going on with time rapidly running out!

People also need to know that while God may allow the problems people are facing in the world, He is not the cause of them. Certainly, Almighty God had the power to stop the rebellion by Satan and one third of the angels. But this would have proved nothing. Instead He chose to grant Satan time to prove the challenge he made against God's Sovereignty and right to rule that would set a universal precedent so that never again would such rank defiance and rebellion ever be tolerated.

God is love and love is the one law that keeps the entire universe functioning in perfect harmony and peace with no place for hatred and greed!

According to the Bible, for a limited time Satan would be the 'ruler of the world.' Notice 1 John 5.19....*the whole world is lying in the power of the wicked one... this is* confirmed in Matthew 4.9 where Jesus was tempted by Satan who showed him all the kingdoms of the world....*all these I will give you for one act of worship 10. To this Jesus replied....Go away Satan for it is written it is Jehovah God you must worship and to him alone give sacred service.*

Going back to the time of Babylon, for the Babylonian Empire the '*Handwriting Was On The Wall.....Daniel 5; 5,25...; MENE, TEKEL and PARSIN. 26. God has numbered the days of your kingdom and has finished it.27 TEKEL...you have been weighed in the balances and 28 PARSIN...your kingdom has been divided and given to the Medes and the Persians. In that very night...Darius the Mede received the kingdom.*

However, this would not be the fate solely of the Babylonian Empire, but would be the fate of all the succeeding world powers since Babylon, right down to our day....all these *forms of ruler-ship have been found deficient according to God's Universal laws and standards.*

Can it honestly be denied that man kinds attempts at self ruler-ship under its present unseen ruler, Satan, Lucifer the Devil or whoever you choose to call him have failed and failed hopelessly...... a sad, sorry and undeniable reality. The preponderance of evidence clearly shows that. ......*To earthling man his way does not belong......even to direct his step* - Jeremiah 10.23..... *man has dominated man to his injury. Ecclesiastes 8;9*

In fact what historians seem to have been missed is that .....according to the Bible, World History is now at an end with no other successive empires or systems mentioned in the Bible, save perhaps a short lived World Government Under the United Nations cited in Revelation 13;14 However, should that happen, it will only last a brief or short period of time with us now being so far into the Biblical *'Final part' of the Last Days.'* Notice Matthew 24; 22...*in fact, unless those days were cut short, no flesh would be saved but on account of the chosen ones...those days will be cut short.*

In a second Book entitled *'A Rush To War'* published in 2011, I suggested that by the War in Iraq lasting six years instead of the planned six months, followed by the financial market crash in 2008, that still lingers on in many countries, that this had actually *bought the world time, a reprieve* by delaying the planned implementation and establishment of the World Order Government the was due to come into effect soon after the Iraq War through what went by the name *The New American Century*. So, hopefully when and if it does come, it will be of very short duration and hopefully this will spare humanity much untold grief and suffering.

However, I digress, if anything, most have abandoned religion with the number of people who describe themselves as 'non religious' or Atheists growing. In 2010 an Australian clergyman lamented that" that the last 40 years or so has seen a wholesale abandonment of the Christian faith."

In France, once a Catholic stronghold Catholicism is in a state of "near collapse" according to the magazine 'The Economist.' Percentagewise Ireland is now among the top 10 atheist populations with news reports talking about the end of Catholic Ireland.

These are just a few notes from the 2010 Global Index of Religion and Atheism published by Gallup International from Polls involving 57 countries representing 73 percent of the world's population. In the United States thousands of Christian churches close down every year with about 1 in 5 people claiming to be Christian.

Regarding false teachings Jesus warned *"by their fruits you will recognize them....every good tree produces fine fruit, but every rotten tree produces worthless fruit."* Matthew 7; 15- 18. Worthless fruit would include political meddling and practices that would offend God. Also, substituting hollow rituals and empty traditions for wholesome teachings found in the Scriptures. "Feed my sheep" Jesus said (John 21;17.}

As a result, today most people are spiritually starved and yet they reject the abundance of spiritual food freely available through the *faithful and discreet slave charged by the master to make available the right food at the proper time*....Matthew 24; 45 – 50. In many instances, this would be as a result of Christendom's efforts to silence the preaching work. In need you can find answers to all your questions on the internet site; www.jw.org.

But there is a sure hope for the future, notice Isaiah 2; 2 – 4 *"and it must occur in the final part of the days that the mountain of the house of Jehovah will become firmly established above the top of the mountains....... And to it all nations must stream."3. And many peoples will...say "Come ,...let us go up to the mountain of Jehovah, to the house of the God of Jacob; and he will instruct us in his ways, and we will walk in his paths." For out of Zion law will go forth, and the word of Jehovah out of Jerusalem."4. And he will certainly render judgment among the nations and set matters straight respecting many peoples, And they will have to beat their swords into plowshares and their spears into pruning shears. Nation will not lift sword against nation, neither will they learn war anymore."*

This foretells that Jehovah God's pure worship will be exalted after centuries of Christendom's apostasy. This would also be the time when Jesus' brothers who had died faithful would be resurrected into the 'Holy of Holies. Daniel 9;24, Revelation 6:11& 14; 4.

By the fourth century A.D. that wily old serpent Satan the Devil, had brought forth his masterpiece of deception, the apostate religion of Christendom – a Babylonian system of worship, hidden under a 'Christian' veneer. It is the principal part of the seed of the Serpent that has developed into a multitude of conflicting sects. Like unfaithful Judah of old, Christendom carries a heavy bloodguilt having been deeply involved on both sides in the first and second World Wars.

1914 would also be a time for those on earth to be measured according to divine standards to qualify for a permanent place in the temple arrangement as spirit-begotten sons of God. – these are ones who would be fully aware of those holy standards and would be determined to measure up Revelation 7; 1 – 3.

Notice Malachi 1;1 - 3.*Suddenly there will come to His temple the [true] Lord who you people are seeking, 3...and he must sit as a refiner and cleanser of silver and he must cleanse the sons of Levi {the priesthood} and clarify them as gold and like silver and they will certainly become to Jehovah a people presenting a gift offering. At that time those in fear of Jehovah spoke with one another... Jehovah kept paying attention and a book of remembrance began to be written up ...for those in fear of Jehovah and for those thinking upon his name.18. And you will ...certainly see a distinction between a righteous one and a wicked one, between one serving God and ne who has not served him.*

A period of forty two months is mentioned in Revelation 11 verse 2 and this period would extend from October 1914 into 1918 and would be a time when all professing Christian clergy would be put to a severe test. Would they uphold Jehovah God's righteous standards during those war years? Most did not en bloc the clergy of Christendom put nationalism ahead of obedience to divine law and on both sides the clergy preached young men into the trenches with millions slaughtered and thus incurred a blood guilt that still cries out for divine vengeance. 1 Peter 4;17. Their being cast out has become permanent, irreversible. Isaiah 59; 1-3, 7,8. Jeremiah 19; 3,4.

What though of the small group of Bible Students who for many years had been preaching the significance of 1914? They were given to the nations to be severely tested. Revelation 11;2. Many realized that they ought not go out and kill their fellowman, but some did not appreciate Christian neutrality and when under pressure from the nations, some compromised.

Zechariah 4; 6,10- 8;9 speaks about *'the day of small beginnings'* and how Jehovah God's purposes are carried out *'not by military force nor by power, but by my spirit. Jehovah of armies has said.'* So it was that from humble beginnings that a small band of Bible Students who had been warning about the importance of 1914 since the mid 1880's persisted and carried the light of truth to mankind during the First World War and as they were, would learn to rely on Jehovah God's strength and would go against the flow of Christendom's opposition and their outrage and use of war hysteria to try to stop the preaching work.

Between 1914 and 1918 they warned of a spiritual drought and the *'coming of the great and fear inspiring day of Jehovah.'* Malachi 4; 1,5 and Amos 8;11 and exposed the death dealing quality of the 'waters' that Christendom was serving to her flocks. Revelation 11; 6.

The present plight of organized religion would have been hard to believe until recently, yet the Bible told about this hundreds of years ago when John wrote the Book of Revelation using symbolic language in Revelation 17; 1-5.

While claiming to represent the Almighty God and Creator, the world's religions have kept company with the "the Kings of the earth" to gain wealth and power........the title Babylon is fitting because of their many false religious teachings and practices, such as triune gods, the immortality of the soul, purgatory, occultism and others that had their roots in Nimrod's ancient Babylon. – Isaiah 47; 1, 8 – 11.

Notice God's warning to people who are disturbed by what is going on in religion today found in Revelation 18;4.."**Get out of her my people**" *if you do not want to share with her in her sins and receive part of her plagues. 23. No light of lamp will ever shine in you again...no voice of groom or bride will ever be heard in you again....for by your spiritistic practices all the nations were misled. 24. Yes, in her was found the blood of prophets and of holy ones and of all those who have been slaughtered on the earth.*

When Babylon the Great is destroyed (by the political system and her wealth plundered) no harm will come to those who have obediently fled her in order to worship the Father in spirit and truth and share the hope of seeing the earth "filled with the knowledge of Jehovah as the waters cover the sea." – Isaiah 11;9.

What this shows is that from small beginnings Jehovah God would put in place a people to uphold His Name and His Sovereignty and right to rule as Creator despite every attempt by the 'wicked one' and those under his influence to stop it!

In the spring of 1918, during the war years when nationalistic feelings were running high, the religious enemies of the witnesses took advantage of the situation through the legal system legal and by legal maneuvering had members of the Watch Tower Society imprisoned on false charges of sedition, effectively putting an end to the preaching work.

Notice how this comes across in Revelation 11; 7 – 10 ' *....when they had finished their witnessing, the wild beast that ascends out of the abyss will make war with them and will kill them'* by putting a stop to the preaching work. The 'wild beast that ascends out of the abyss' – is the world's political system under Satan's control. This can be seen at Daniel 7; 2,3,17.

Notice Revelation 11: 15 *'And the seventh angel blew his trumpet. And loud voices occurred in heaven saying; 'The kingdom of the world did become the kingdom of our Lord and of his Christ, and he will rule as king forever and ever.*

This is a vital historic announcement of universal importance that should be of concern to every living soul with us now being so far into the 'last days.'

Then there is the sworn declaration by the strong angel in Revelation 10; 16,7.; *"There will be no delay any longer."* As the Messianic King, Jesus will fulfill Jehovah's Word and vindicate his Father's Universal Sovereignty as "The King of eternity who must rule as Sovereign Lord"

In the United States during 1918-1919 and through the 1920's, the 1930's and beyond the witnesses exposed Christendom's crafty dabbling in politics and especially the Catholic hierarchy's accords made with the fascist and Nazi dictator's. In response the clergy framed mischief by law and organized mob violence against God's people and fellow workers. Notice how this comes across in Psalm 94...verse 20. *Will the throne causing adversities be allied with you while they are framing trouble by decree? 21...They make sharp attacks on the soul of the righteous one and pronounce wicked even the blood of the innocent one.....23. But Jehovah....will turn back upon them their hurtfulness and will silence them with their own calamity.*

The kingdom good news had to be preached. Errors had to be exposed, lost sheep had to be found and the world was forced to sit up and take notice. In obedience to the angels trumpet blasts the witnesses continued to expose Christendom as deserving of Jehovah' adverse judgments.

A Convention of the Bible Students in London, England May 25 – 31, 1926 featured a resolution 'A testament to the 'Rulers of the World' and a public talk on 'Why World Powers are Failing - The Remedy a complete text of both of these was published by a leading London newspaper the following day. Later 50 million tracts about the resolution was distributed worldwide – years later people in England still spoke of the stinging expose'. At the convention a new book Deliverance was released proving that the 'man child' government, Christ's heavenly kingdom had been born in 1914. (Matthew 24; 3-14, Luke 21; 24-26 and Revelation 12; 1 – 10.

Thereafter it quoted a manifesto published in London in 1918 and signed by eight clergymen who were from *Baptist, Congregational, Presbyterian, Episcopalian, Methodist and other Protestant denominations. The manifesto proclaimed that the 'present crisis pointed toward the close of the time of the Gentiles' and that the revelation of the Lord may* be expected at any moment. These clergy had recognized the signs of Jesus' presence!

The book *Deliverance* informs; 'The most remarkable part of the affair was that the very men who signed the manifesto subsequently repudiated it and rejected the evidence proving that we are at the end of the world and in the day of the Lord's second presence.'

Rather than announce the incoming Kingdom of God, Christendom's clergy have chosen to remain as part of Satan's world. They wanted no part with the small band of Bible Students and their King!

'They have over them a king the angel of the abyss. In Hebrew his name is Abaddon (Destruction) but in Greek Apollyon (Destroyer) Revelation 9;11.

3. SOMETHING THAT HAS BEEN GOING ON IN AMERICA AND IN THE WORLD THAT FEW ARE AWARE OF

Notice how America, once the 'Land of the Free' is described in Revelation Chapter 13 verse 11.......*and I saw another wild beast ascending out of the earth and it had two horns like a lamb, but it began speaking as a dragon.*

This shows how the 'wicked one' would ultimately find a way to twist America into becoming law-enforcer to Rome and the coming Global Fascist (Church) State or World Government. As such the Bible is correct when it tells that America would begin speaking like a dragon – a Devil.

Perhaps this would be the reason why the Muslim World refers to America as the 'Great Satan.' But more about that in the Chapter dealing more fully with Revelation Chapter 13.

It should not surprise that as 'Ruler of the World,' the wicked one would position himself behind the world's greatest Country and behind the world's largest 'Christian' Church or religion to achieve his aims and ultimate purpose of world domination.

The next few chapters will provide the facts about what has been going on behind the scene in America that generally people know little about and urgently need to know and will also explain why so much is done to keep folk from knowing the truth about what is really going on in the world.

The general lowering of standards in today's 'anything goes,' society, without going into detail, spelling out the widespread moral decay and corruption, clearly shows our world's ruler-ship or governance has failed hopelessly! Or more particularly that it is in fact Satan's failed system. He is referred to in the Bible as the 'ruler of the world'; *The Evil One controls the whole world' 1 John 5;19.*

Again, with so few prophecies yet to be fulfilled, how did this situation arise? Notice the following;

Created in God' image and likeness ours should be system based on love because God is love. In fact this is the law of the universe, the 'law of one', something that science refers to as the 'unified field theory,' all energy being one, the same energy that controls and keeps the entire universe in complete and harmony with the exception, for a limited time, of planet earth, a time that will soon end.

To understand this it needs to be realized that everything from the tiniest molecule to a brick wall, including our bodies is simply energy vibrating at different frequencies. In fact what we see is simply reflected light. Turn off the light and there is just darkness. Light waves or photons that reach our eyes are in fact received upside down and are turned right side up by the brain that interprets the images.

Similarly our ears receive sound waves between a range of between 27 beats per second and 20,000 bps. A piano by comparison produces sound waves only up to 4000 bps.

These are just two examples to illustrate what and who we really are. It has been said that the DNA of all 7 billion people on earth would be little more than just a film on a teaspoon. So, clearly intelligent design, now very much everywhere in evidence, confirms that our Creator actually does have 'the whole world in His hands.'

Normally people want to be peaceable, honest and kind. Why, then is there so much crime, violence, injustice, cruelty and all the other ills, despite mankind having reached such an advanced stage of technological development? Why has mankind been unable to solve the problems of crime, violence and poverty?

Did God make humans with an evil tendency? No, humans were created in God's image, with the desire to imitate His love Genesis 1:27, Job 34:10. God dignified the human family with free will, but under the influence of the 'wicked one' mankind rejected God and became imperfect.

Notice what is written in Deuteronomy 32......"Give ear, O heavens and let me speak (Moses wrote Deuteronomy) *verse 3. For I shall declare the name of God. Do you attribute greatness to our God! 4. The Rock, perfect is his activity, for all his ways are justice. A God of faithfulness, with whom there is no injustice; Righteous and upright is he. 5. They have acted ruinously on their part. They are not his children, the defect is their own, A generation crooked and twisted. 6. It is to your God that you keep doing this. O people stupid and not wise. Is he not your Father who has produced you, He who made you and proceeded to give you stability.*

So, created in God's image we should be like him, kind and loving. Yet, why is the opposite the case with man driven by selfishness and greed, seemingly hell bent on destroying both himself and his domain?

What was created as a self-sustaining paradise home for the human family that if properly appreciated and cared for would continue indefinitely, is rapidly reaching a stage where it's destruction will soon be beyond repair, with the rape and plunder of the earth and its resources continuing with ineffective steps being taken to rectify matters. Will it be a case of too little, too late? Save that only by Divine intervention matters will be rectified as is clearly prophesied in Scripture.

Matthew 24.14 puts it this way.....*this good news of the Kingdom will be preached in all the earth and **then the end will come**, it's that simple! Certainly the preaching work, now at an advance stage, has happened despite untold efforts to stop it.*

However, it would seem that in the euphoria of victory after World War ll, the American people were taken off guard. Unable to destroy these ones, 'God's people' in two world wars provided Satan with an opportunity to change tactics.

After suffering defeat in both World Wars, for the 'wicked one' it was a case of...... "*If you can't beat them, join them.*"How?

By quietly infiltrating his kind, those under his influence into the world's two great Protestant nations he would change tactics and take them down from within, primarily through what is known as Ecumenism, a crafty deceptive; '*let's all get along and forget our differences*'device and strategy that would be used by the Jesuits to destroy Protestantism, with the Jesuits behind the scene overjoyed as they put it," watching Protestantism in its '*death throes.*'

This infiltration of America would not be confined only to religion, but in fact would be all encompassing and would involve pretty much every aspect of what is the American way. The Catholic Church through it's schools and universities would focus on taking control of the human resource areas in both the private and public sectors by churning out Human Resource Managers who would ensure that priority was given to the employment of the laity over a wide front, albeit that it would be done using a 'step by step' approach, a slow but sure method to the end of the Church entrenching itself and gaining control of large parts of both America's private and public sectors.

A small but extremely important example of this can be seen in them makeup of the membership of the U.S. Supreme Court until recently with; ....Justices - Roberts, Kennedy, Scalia, Thomas & Alito.... five in number or (56%) – who are Catholics. As such for the first time in U.S. history, Catholics became the majority in the U.S. Justice system. However, this could change following the death of Justice Scalia whose successor has yet to be confirmed.

How could this not influence judicial decisions across America and in fact corrupt and destroy the fidelity, integrity and the very fabric of the entire Justice System of the United States? Again, this is just one small example to show what has been going on. For all intents and purposes it could be said that America is now pretty much a Catholic country.

The Vatican with its vast wealth and resources would use these to gain control of any company it deemed necessary simply by obtaining a significant shareholding in that particular company or institution to ensure that Board members and executives would include enough Catholics to influence its decisions. Call this methodology company/country capture!

U.S. Immigration is another area where through the appointment of Judges and other officials priority would be given to ensuring that immigrants from South, Central America and Mexico, the majority being Catholic's, would gain entry and ultimately citizenship to help influence decisions at the polls.

Similarly, attention would also be given to ensuring that Catholics gained positions of power and authority in both law enforcement and in the military.

Interestingly of the 45 Declared Communist Goals for The 'Take-Over' of America written into the United States Congressional Record in 1963. See www.Rense.com only one goal remains to be achieved, goal number 11, for a World Government to be put in place through the United Nations. Which very likely will follow the recent Cope 21 Climate Change Conference in Paris.

Going through all 45 points will show in detail how and what has facilitated the moral breakdown of America and also show how the American people are being and have over a long period been deceived and conned into giving up their hard fought and God given freedom and liberty.

One might argue that these were once the goals solely of America's Communist Party, but if one were to look closer into how and by whom they have been implemented following the demise of the Soviet Union, a clearer picture will emerge showing how these too, it would seem have been high jacked to serve 'a greater cause' namely, for the takeover of America.

The World Government that is almost upon us, will not come about through a vote at the ballot box! All such freedom and liberty will then be a thing of the past. Instead for the majority of people it will be them becoming some kind of mind controlled robot. Notice the following;

'The Constitution of the U.S.S.R. is almost identical to the Constitution of the United Nations....' All nations will be brought under it's, the U.N.'s 'iron-fisted' fascist control.

Fourth Reich of the Rich. Emissary Publishers, South Pasadena, Ca

1978 p.140 .

No one will enter the New World Order unless he or she will make a pledge to worship Lucifer. No one will enter the New Age unless he will take a Luciferian initiation. The light reveals to us the presence of the Christ comes from Lucifer. He is the light-giver, he is aptly named the 'Morning Star' because it is his light that heralds for man the dawn of a great consciousness.

By contrast the Bible chooses to call him the 'father of the lie' John 8.44.

So, how could this possibly characterize the UN which supposedly was setup to end wars and bring peace and security to all nations?

People need to know that the United Nations was actually brought into existence by the Illuminati. They had tried and failed with the League of Nations after World War l and so they engineered the Second World War to batter nations into agreeing to replace it with the United Nations. They wrote the charter that would make the UN a stalking horse for a fully-fledged world government.

Also, noteworthy is that the Illuminati's control of money translates into them controlling the world. The problems of poverty, debt, war are made to happen because it makes humanity easier to control. That just 1% of American's now control 99% of its wealth clearly shows how complete is this control.

There have even been some very sobering reports that the U.S. Military establishment is preparing for a Third World War as early as in 2016, before the expiry of President Obama's term of office, possibly this is deemed necessary in the face of the growing strength and sophistication of the Chinese and Russian military and necessary for America to retain its supremacy and primarily to ensure that the Illuminati's goal for the establishment of a World Government will succeed!

Might this be a wake-call for folk to start seeing and taking very seriously what is really going on in the world and also to properly understand and expose the churches involvement which is key in the entire saga? Why, because understanding and knowing what is going on might save your very life!

4. SOME LITTLE KNOW FACTS ABOUT WORLD WAR ll

Hitler's Vice Chancellor was a Baron von Papen, a Papal Knight and a good Catholic and it was he that signed the Concordant with the Vatican and without him Hitler very likely would never have received the support of Germany's industrial leader's and the high moral support of the Church.

The following is a brief review of the facts behind Hitler's rise to power in Germany and the role played by the church.

- In May 1924 the Nazi Party held 32 seats in the German Reichstag.

-By May 1928 these had dwindled to 12 seats.

However riding in the wake of the Great Depression the Nazis made a remarkable recovery, gaining 230 out of the 608 seats in July 1932.

Soon after this, former Chancellor Franz von Papen, a Papal Knight, came to the Nazis aid. According to historians, von Papen envisioned a new Holy Roman Empire. By January 1933, he had mustered support for Hitler from Germany's industrial barons, and through wily intrigues he ensured that Hitler became Germany's Chancellor on January 30, 1933.

He was made Vice Chancellor and was used by Hitler to win the support of Catholics in Germany. Within two months of gaining power, Hitler dissolved Parliament and dispatched thousands of opposition leaders to concentration camps and began an open campaign of oppressing the Jews and others.

On July 20, 1933 Cardinal Pacelli, who later became Pope Pius XII signed a Concordant in Rome between the Vatican and Nazi Germany. Von Papen signed the document as Hitler's representative and the Pope conferred on von Papen the Grand Cross of the Order of Pius.

In his book *Satan in Top Hat*, Tiber Koeves states "The Concordant was a great victory for Hitler. It gave him the first moral support he had received from the outside world, and this from the most exalted source."

However, after the Concordant was signed...it was never observed by the Nazi Party and a long and persistent persecution of the Catholic Church, its priesthood and its members was carried out. The Vatican's earnest protests made to Von Ribbentrop were never answered. Nuremberg: IMT 1947 pp 98 – 102 before Justice Jackson. (The Nazi Party was predominantly anti-Christian and irreligious. In 1941 Martin Bormann had issued a secret decree to suppress the influence of the church over the state to secure the Reich.)

By the end of 1933 (proclaimed a "Holy Year" by Pope Pius XI) Vatican support had become a major factor in Hitler's push for **world domination**. Though a handful of priests and nuns protested against Hitler's atrocities - and suffered for it - the Vatican as well as the Catholic Church gave either active or tacit support to the Nazi tyranny, which they regarded as a bulwark against the advance of communism. The holocaust went un-criticized by Pope Pius XII.

In September 1939 in a pastoral letter the German Catholic bishops wrote..." In this decisive hour we admonish our Catholic soldiers to do their duty in obedience to the Fueher........".we appeal to the Faithful to join in ardent prayers that Divine Providence may lead this war to blessed success."

Churchill in his book *The Gathering Storm 1948* notes that Hitler appointed von Papen as German minister in Vienna for "*the undermining or winning over of leading personalities in Austrian politics.*" Churchill quotes the U.S. minister in Vienna as saying of von Papen; "*In the boldest and most cynical manner von Papen proceeded to tell me that...he intended to use his reputation as a good Catholic to gain influence with Austrians like Cardinal Innitzer.*"

After Austria had capitulated and Hitler's storm troopers had goose-stepped into Vienna, Catholic Cardinal Innitzer ordered all Austrian churches to fly the Swastika flag, ring their bells, pray for Adolf Hitler in honor of his birthday.

Surely, this provides an example of how Satan's has used and manipulated religion for his own purposes, even Christianity which clearly is part of Satan's worldwide empire of false religion, which in the Book of Revelation is called,' Babylon the Great.'

Certainly, it has not been God's instrument for bringing peace to the earth. Rather she has served "the kings of the earth" with whom she commits religious fornication. Notice this in Revelation Chapter 17 verse 1... "*Come I will show you the judgment of the great prostitute....2. with whom the kings of the earth have committed immorality...5 And on her forehead was written a name of mystery "Babylon the Great, mother of harlots and of the earth's abominations. 6. And I saw the woman drunk with the blood of the saints and the martyrs of Jesus – (The Church Inquisition....)*

Notice in Revelation 18.4 the call from Heaven to...."*Come out of her **my people** or share with her in her sins and if you do not want to receive part of her plagues.*" And further in verse 23; *no light of lamp will ever shine in you again and no voice of bride or groom will ever be heard in you again; because ....by your spiritistic practices all nations were misled. 24 Yes, in her was found the blood of prophets and of holy ones and of all those who have been slaughtered on the earth.*"

Certainly her doctrines and enslaving practices have kept and continue to keep the masses passively subservient to their rulers. Call it a 'prison religion' with the laity not permitted even to read the Bible leaving over a billion people held in blind and passive submissive obedience.

In fact the 'wicked ones, intent has been to keep everyone in bondage and enslavement through money, politics and religion.

It should also be apparent how Satan has used Germany twice as an instrument to try to bring about the destruction and demise of the British and American people, who in the Bible, God refers to as 'My People' and that it has only been through the Divine hand of Protection during their long history since crossing the Red Sea that they have survived. It also shows that Satan is not all knowing and cannot see the future, he simply backed the loser twice!

Yet, this all seems to be of little concern and even forgotten by the majority today and has been conveniently swept under the proverbial rug.

Why did the church not take Britain or America's side of the issue? Well, Britain was not a Catholic country and was struggling economically trying to recover from the staggering cost of the WWI. While, America had not yet gained recognition as a Super Power and was still in the 'backwaters,' geopolitically speaking. It was only after the war that she would become a Super Power.

In those pre-war days Europe was regarded as the world's center of culture and civilization, with Berlin, Vienna, Rome, Paris and other European cities magnets to the elite. Using Darwin's thesis on the survival of the species, Hitler envisioned the German people becoming a super breed, a Master Race, a pure Aryan Nation, while discriminating against Jews, Poles, Blacks and others as *'untermens,'* sub-humans. The Vatican saw in Hitler a way to re-establish her former glory through a new 'Holy Roman Empire.'

Certainly the Bible and Religious practice today are poles apart. So much is done in the name of religion that simply cannot be approved of by God. The wars of the past century provide an excellent example showing religious elements on both sides encouraging their people to engage in warfare. Protestants killing Protestants, Catholics killing Catholics. Instead of being a force for peace, religion has promoted war and killing.

Catholic historian E.I Watkin acknowledged:

"Painful as the admission must be, we cannot in the interests of false edification or dishonest loyalty deny or ignore the historical fact that Bishops have consistently supported wars waged by the government of their country"..."What war was ever fought in which God was claimed to be on both sides?

5. REVELATION CHAPTER 13

This Chapter is key to helping people understand the prophecy's about what is going on in the world during, these the 'final part' of the 'last days' and also to learn the identity of the Biblical characters involved and more importantly to know about a World Order Government that will soon be put in place through the United Nations;

Revelation 13.2......the dragon (Satan) gave to the wild beast (the Papacy) its power and its throne and great authority. 3. And I saw one of its head's as though slaughtered to death, but its death-stroke got healed....

Revelation 13.8......... and all the earth will worship it (the wild beast); <u>the name of not one of them stands written in the scroll of life</u> of the Lamb who was slaughtered from the founding of the world.

He, the 'wicked one' might be powerful but certainly he is not Almighty as is the Creator, Almighty God the God of true prophecy! Certainly Satan cannot see the future otherwise he surely would have seen the futility of backing the loosing side in both World Wars.

Further in Revelation Chapter 13 verse 11 notice more about the coming World Government and the various Biblical characters involved in its formation; again verse 11.....*I saw another wild beast,).....it had two horns like a lamb, but began speaking as a dragon (America in a new role as law enforcer to Rome and a World Order government). 12. And it makes the earth and those that dwell in it worship the first wild beast (the Papacy), whose death stroke got healed.*

Here we see America, more specifically the Anglo-American world power in a new role as the Biblical false prophet. Notice that while it at one time it spoke like a lamb that it would begin speaking like a dragon – a devil! This is today's America after being taken down from within and made 'law-enforcer' to Rome!

14. *It misleads those who dwell on the earth and tells them to make an image to the wild beast (the Papacy) whose death stroke got healed. The image would be a Fascist World Government through the United Nations - fascism being rule by one man (the Papacy).*

15. And it will *cause to be killed all those who will not worship the image of the wild beast.*

16. *And it puts under compulsion all persons, the small and the great, the rich and the poor....that they should give these a mark on their right hand or upon their forehead....*

17. *that nobody might be able to buy or sell except persons having the mark, the name of the wild beast or the number of its name.... a man's number 666.*

The letters inscribed on the Pope's miter are these 'Vicarius Fili Dei' which translated from Latin is VICAR OF THE SON OF GOD. By adding up the letters of this name using Roman numerals, the number of the name will be 666.

Our Sunday Visitor, April 18, 1915

Vicarius - 'Substituting for or in the place of...'

V I C A R I U S

5 + 1 + 100 + 0 + 0 + 1 + 5 + 0 = 112

F   I   L   I   I

0 + 1 + 50 + 1 + 1 =   53

D   E   I

500 + 0 + 1 = 501

666

Notice a warning about accepting the mark found further in Revelation Chapter 14. 9.....*If anyone worships the wild beast and its image and receives its mark....10, he will also, drink of the wine of the anger of God.....12. Here is where it means endurance for the holy ones, those who observe the commandments of God and have faith in Jesus (His Ransom Sacrifice.)*

How can telling this not be in the very best interests of every living soul, are we not all family, God's human family that our common enemy Satan so desperately wants to destroy?

Why? Simply because he knows his time is up and that he is destined to go into destruction and wants to take all humanity down with him to leave God with an empty victory!

Yet, it is something that the world's controlled media, its political, educational and theocratic systems choose to ignore! Not a word is said or allowed to be said about it.

So great is this Satanically inspired deception that it can only be described as the '*curse of ignorance. "How so, one might ask?"*

The answer would simply be that Satan deceives, that's what he does to even his own and he does it well.

Sadly, our elite, our deluded would be Masters in the New World Order have yet to realize that they too have been deceived. Again, as already mentioned, when Satan goes down he intends taking all humanity down with him, them included!

Well, that is only part of the story, but sufficient to show that there definitely is something going on, without going into how those who refuse to bow down to the beast will be rounded up and how fully staffed concentration camps are already in existence and ready both in the United States and around the world .....one that recently mentioned in the news was Australia's Christmas Island 'Immigration ' facility that was set on fire by the inmates.

No doubt the privately owned immigration detention centers that also featured recently in financial news highlighting their exceptional profits, would also be part of this arrangement.

But, let's see what the Bible says about America in it's new role as an aggressor nation or power; first we go to Daniel Chapter 11 in verse 40.

Here America is referred by another name... please follow along....*And in the time of the end the king of the south will engage with him (the king of the north) in a pushing....*

Clearly, America as King of the South is shown here as the aggressor, the one doing the pushing without going further and showing the results.

In Jeremiah chapter 5, because of Israel's treacherous dealings with God the prophet tells how God will react....15. *"here I am bringing in upon you a nation from far away ....a nation of long ago, a nation whose language you cannot understand...17. They will certainly eat your harvest...eat up your flocks and your herds. They will shatter your fortified cities in which you are trusting. 18. in those days 19. Just as you have left me and gone serving a foreign god in your land, so you will serve strangers in a land that is not yours. 20 Tell it all to the House of Jacob. The following chapter will show the modern day identity of Jacob.*

6. HAS THE IDENTITY OF MODERN DAY ISRAEL BEEN SUPRESSED?

Identifying who Israel is today is key to understanding Bible prophecy, especially prophecy about the last days!

The Bible Book of Geneses shows that Abraham had two sons, Ishmael and Isaac and that Ishmael would be father to the Arab nations or twelve sheiks of Ishmael and that Isaac through his son Jacob, whose name God changed to Israel would be father to the twelve tribes of Israel.

And certainly, while there does not seem to be any problem identifying today's Arab peoples as the descendants of Ishmael, the same cannot be said about identifying today's Anglo American peoples as descendants of Jacob and his son Joseph's, two Egyptian born sons Ephraim and Manasseh. In fact this appears to have been swept under the proverbial rug.

Certainly, when the Bible mentions Israel in prophecy's about the last days it is not referring solely to the Modern Jewish state of Israel, occupying a strip of land along the coast of Palestine.

In Geneses Chapter 48 it will be noted that when his father Jacob (Israel) was dying his son Joseph brought his two Egyptian born sons, Ephraim and Manasseh to their grand-father's bedside to be blessed. As such they would inherit all the Abramic 'Birthright' promises that would be withheld 'seven times' on account of Israel's repeated disobedience, but would eventually be faithfully delivered by their righteous God.

Notice more about this as we continue in verse 16 of Genesis Chapter 48.....*Let my name (Israel) be called upon them and the name of my father's Abraham and Isaac and let them increase to a multitude in the midst of the earth*, the boys Ephraim the youngest and Manasseh the oldest. Verses 17 –

shows that while Manasseh would become a great nation the younger one Ephraim would become the greater of the two.

Undeniably, the Bible from Genesis to Revelation is the history of God's dealings with one nation, the Nation of Israel. It is the, English speaking people of the world and not simply the Jews that have inherited the birthright promises made to Abraham, Isaac and Jacob. Whatis not appreciated today is that the Jews (tribe of Judah) was only a part of the Twelve Tribe nation of Israel. Certainly Judah was a part of Israel, but not all Israelites are Jews!

Understanding who Israel is a major key to understanding the Bible and the prophecies written for our day.

In Jeremiah Chapter 51 God actually shows his indignation for the people of the nations in verse 17 where they are described as builders of *'images of falsehood'* while in verse 20. it is said of His chosen people Israel....*'thou art my battle axe and weapons of war; for with thee will I break in pieces the nations, and with thee I will destroy kingdoms.'*

This should in any way detract from the New Testament writings and the Apostle Paul who as a chosen vessel was tasked with taking the Good News of God's Kingdom to the nation's and to bring into the Christian congregation people from the nations to share in God's Salvation arrangement through Christ!

However, Paul's writings in the Book of Roman's in Chapter 11, clearly explains that God's covenant with Israel would nevertheless continue to time indefinite. This was done through an illustration of an olive tree with branches (people of the nations) being grafted in.

Notice what the 'birthright' blessing or inheritance would be;

Genesis 22;17...*I shall surely ....multiply you like the grains of sand on the seashore....and your seed will take possession of the gates of his enemy – (strategic gates like Gibraltar, Suez, Straits of Singapore, Leyte Gulf etc.)*

Genesis 28.14 Abraham's son Isaac is blessed....'*and you will certainly spread abroad to the west, to the east, to the north and to the south and by your seed all families will certainly bless themselves.'*

Genesis 27 verse 28....and may the true God give you the Dews of the Heavens and the Fertile soils of the earth and an abundance of grain and new wine.29. let national groups bow low to you...become master over your brothers....cursed be anyone cursing you and blessed those blessing you.

Genesis 35.10...*no longer is your name to be called Jacob, but Israel. 11. Be fruitful and become many, nations and a congregation (Commonwealth?) of nations will proceed out of you, and kings will come out of your loins.*

Put into perspective and without explaining Israel's incredible migration out of the middle east to the British Isles and beyond, might it be asked where in all history has there ever been a co-existing Great Nation and a Company or Common Wealth of nations possessing the Gates of their enemies, strategic possessions like Suez, Gibraltar, Panama and others who would enjoy possession of the 'most fertile soils of the earth.' Britain, America, Canada, Australia, New Zealand, South Africa, India and other lands.

A colonizing people spread out around the earth to the north, south, east and west.

A people with a long line of kings, a people dwelling in places of permanent security and yet always at war.

A people possessing the choicest parts of the earth who despite at times being vastly outnumbered have through

Divine Providence always prevailed? History is full of such examples; the Armada, Trafalgar, Waterloo, Dunkirk, the battle of Britain, El Alamein, ...Normandy, Midway, Coral Sea. The list is endless.

After the Battle of Leyte Gulf, U.S. Operational Commander Sprague was astounded...He had held his own against a fleet many times stronger...He later wrote that his success was not simply due to tactics, but also to the 'definite partiality of Almighty God.'

Similarly, General Dwight D. Eisenhower, Supreme Commander of Allied Forces during Normandy Operation remarked..."If there was nothing else in my life to prove the existence of an Almighty and Merciful God, the events of the next 24 hours did!"

From virtual obscurity at the beginning of the 18th Century Britain – Ephraim and later America – Manasseh emerged on to the world scene to take positions where in a short space of time they collectively controlled almost three quarters of the most productive land of the world.

It was through Abraham's faith that these unconditional promises that had to be fulfilled if God's word was to be found true, were bestowed upon him and his heirs.

While the Bible tells much about Abraham's son Isaac and also Jacob what does it tell about Ishmael and for that matter Jacob's son Esau?

A brief account of this is as follows;(Regarding Hager's son Ishmael) ....in Genesis 16.1 we read....*Sarai, (Sarah) Abram's (Abraham) wife had borne no children, but she had an Egyptian maidservant and her name was Hagar. 3. Sarah...gave her to Abram 4. ....she became pregnant (by Abram) 6.....Then Sarah began to humiliate her so she ran away. 7. Later God's angel found her. 9 "return to your mistress and humble yourself" 10. Then God's angel said to* her; "I shall greatly multiply your son and you must call his name Ishmael."[Father of the Arab Nations] 12. ....As for him, he will become a Zebra of a man. His hand will be against everyone and everyone's hand will be against him; and before the face of his brothers he will tabernacle.

After the death of Mohammed in 632 A.D. the Arabs had carried the Sword of Islam from the Atlantic Ocean across North Africa, Egypt, Arabia, the Holy Land, Armenia, Persia and Afghanistan.

The Empire of the Arabs was larger than that of Alexander the Great and Rome and for 500 years it carried the torch of civilization.

In Genesis 17; 19-21 we read...I will make you a great nation (Ishmael) but my Covenant I will establish with Israel.

In time Abraham was to have other children, but in Genesis 25;5 we note...'Abraham gave everything he had to Isaac.'

Turning to Genesis chapter 25 provides an account of how Isaac's wife Rebekah became pregnant. We pick up the story in verse 22....the sons within her began to struggle with each other...23...God proceeded to say to her "two nations are in your belly, and two national groups will be separated from your inward parts, the one national group will be stronger than the other and the older will serve the younger.

In verse 27 we read....Esau (the older) became a hunter a man of the field, but Jacob (a blameless man), dwelling in tents.

Verse 28.tells that...Isaac had love for Esau because it meant game in his mouth.

However, as the story continues notice what would happen between the two brothers as regards the birthright promises; 29.Jacob was making stew when Esau came along from the field and he was tired. 30. So Esau said to Jacob "Quick *please, give me a swallow of the red – the red there, for I am tired." 31. To this Jacob said "Sell me, first your right as firstborn!" 32. Esau continued; "here I am simply going to die, and of what benefit to me is a birthright? 33. And Jacob added; "Swear to me first of all!" And he proceeded to swear to him and sell his right as firstborn to Jacob.*

34. So Esau despised his birthright. At Hebrews 12; 16 we read ..*'that there may be no one not appreciating sacred things like Esau who in exchange for a meal gave away his rights as firstborn.'*

Notice the outcome of the matter later when Isaac was on his deathbed as recorded in Genesis Chapter 27 verse 30 ....*as soon as Isaac had blessed Jacob ..... Esau came back from hunting. 31. Esau said to his father " is there just one blessing you have for me? 39. So Isaac said* **"Behold away from the fertile soils of the earth your dwelling will be.....away from the dew of the heavens"....40. "And by the sword you will live, and your brother you will serve.** <u>**But it will occur when you grow restless, you will indeed Break His Yoke off your Neck.**</u>*"*Is this perhaps something for which modern day Israel, America should take heed?

The above are extracts from my first book entitled 'In God We Trust' published in 2000.

Before Christmas 2005 I took it upon myself to send a copy of the book to all 100 United States Senators without spelling out my concerns and while I was thrilled to receive letters from a few Senator's, there was no indication that the above, which I considered to be a dire warning to America, had been picked up.

The War in Iraq was dragging on with no end in sight and it was my hope that, what I would call it 'a word to the wise' would be in order and that hopefully by going through the book they might give some thought to Genesis chapter 27 verse 40 without spelling out what the implications would be as regards the future relationship of the West, modern day Israel with it's brother Islamic nations.

While I have little or no knowledge of the Koran, I do recall hearing on the radio a few snatches of verses 190 – 192 about Jihad or when/why Islam would wage war. What I took away from it was that a Jihad or holy war would continue until the enemy took it upon himself to seek peace.

My thinking at the time of this writing, now in the year 2016, is that perhaps this was an approach that might have been seriously considered, prior to the development of the current situation. Who knows back then it may have had positive results. Now however it would appear to be too late with international Jihadism so widespread and embedded with the time for the success of such diplomacy seemingly impossible

However, might I add that my view is that when homes, families, businesses, schools, hospitals of peoples, the majority of whom very likely are normal ever-day a-political people are destroyed, by high level surgical bombing that this would evoke outright anger, rage, hatred, resentment to say the least in any nation that likely in their eyes would warrant and justify revenge by any means! Also, surely it puts the lives of Americans everywhere at risk! For certainly violence begets violence.

Surely, now with most countries being heavily populated without the undulating sparsely populated areas that in the past offered ideal 'theatres of war, new ways need urgently to be sought to settle differences without devastating the lives of the innocent majority? Will the unintended cosequences of 'Regime Change' in the Middle East justify the policy? Outside of scriptural thinking what is going on could continue for decades without let up...will it be case of 'so much' for the World Order aspirations of the few behind the scene directing such matters.

The life of Muhammad Ali (Cassius Clay Jr) and his humanity provides an excellent example that could be followed!

Certainly journalists have used the word 'quagmire' to describe the present geopolitical situation of the West in the middle-east, in Syria, Libya, Afghanistan and places that have resulted in huge waves of refugees flowing into Europe where they are not welcomed.

After the Minsk talks with Russia, U.S. Secretary of State John Kerry chose to say that it was now a multi polar world where America was no longer the main player on the international scene.

Hopefully, positive developments will not be long in coming and that fresh thinking in such matters will produced the desired result namely, world peace, before the 'final whistle' blows from on high.

Matthew 24.14 however, does tell that...*the good news of the kingdom will be preached throughout the world then the end will come.* Again, this shows where we are in the stream of time!!

So, we are admonished to keep on the watch in verse 44. *Because at an hour you do not know the Son of man is coming...21. For then there will be great tribulation such as has not occurred since the world's beginning....but on account of the chosen ones those days will be cut short.*

Certainly, this sounds a warning that very soon there will be Divine intervention to sort matters out!

7. ABOUT THE PAPACY - 'HE WILL CHANGE TIME'

In Daniel 7. Verse 25 it is written....*he will change **time** and laws, and they will be given into his hands for a time, times and half a time. (A time being a year or 360 days.)*

According to the Bibles 'day for a year' principle, a time 360 + times 360 + 360 and half a time 180 would equal 1260 years ie.; 360 + 720 + 180 = 1260 years.

This is **Huge**. Once understood the world can never be the same again! A simple calculation will show that the Bible truly is 'history written in advance,' written for our guidance by our kind and loving Heavenly Father, God and Creator.

The legally recognized supremacy of the Pope began in 538 A.D. when there went into effect a decree of Emperor Justinian, making the Bishop of Rome head over all the churches, the definer of doctrine and the corrector of heretics.

Vigilius ascended the papacy in 538 A.D. under the military protection of Baliserius - History of the Christian Church Vol. 3 p.327

However, 1260 years later in 1798 A.D., the murder of a Frenchman in Rome gave Napoleon an excuse for occupying the Eternal City and putting an end to the Papal temporal power. – Church History, p.24.

History shows that in A.D. 1798 a French General Berthier made his entrance into Rome, abolished the Papal

government and established a secular one in it's place. –
The Encyclopedia Anversary 1941 ed.

Europe thought Napoleon's veto would be obeyed and that
the papacy was dead. – Rev Joseph Ricaby – The Modern
Papacy, p. 1.

However, this would not be the end of the Papacy forin 1929
Mussolini and Cardinal Gasppari signed the Italian Vatican
Pact. In terms of the agreement the Pope would receive 750
million Lire for his support of the fascist party. San
Francisco Chronicle Feb 11, 1929.

As such the 'death-stroke' mentioned in Revelation 13.3 was
healed.

So, recorded history confirms and shows that the Papacy
which began in 538 A.D. would last 1260 years (538 + 1260)
and would continue until <u>1798 A.D.</u>

How can something so extremely simple yet so vitally
important be ignored? Also how has this been missed by
theologians, historians, academics and institutions of higher
learning?

Yet, there it is, overwhelming proof and evidence
confirming not only the true identity of the Papacy as the
wild beast in Revelation Chapter 13but also it's direct links
to the 'Great Dragon', Satan the Devil who gives it, it's
throne and great power and authority.

8. HE WILL CHANGE LAWS

Hitherto, religious discussions and efforts by evangelists to persuade an unbeliever, invariably would break down for one reason, the 'Just Believe' response to any request for evidence and proof of the existence of God.

But, certainly the Bible and history do provide such hard evidence which again testifies to the incredible accuracy and truth of the Bible as already shown, but there is more, notice the following;

Little pleasure can be gained in telling another that he has been deceived, or that his religion is wrong, but nevertheless it is that important.

Truth is intolerant of error – it doesn't matter what you think or what I think, what the Bible says is true, however it is for the individual to either accept or reject it!

The Bible discusses Christ and the Anti Christ because these two forces are the forces that will battle it out in the end. What needs to be understood is the role of the antichrist. If we don't understand its role, we won't understand how deception will filter into our systems of worship to make people think what they are involved in is right, when it is actually wrong.

We need to identify the antichrist and keep an 'eye' on what he is doing to see how prophecy is being fulfilled in the Bible.

2 Peter 1.20...no prophecy of Scripture springs from private interpretation. Only the Bible can tell us who the Antichrist is.

AN'TI, n. [Greek. See Ante] means...'in place of' - Websters Dictionary 1828....So clinically speaking it is somebody coming 'in the place of Christ'. Not as it may seem as someone opposed to Christ.

Today, we are told not to worry about the antichrist, and that Christ will destroy him. That may well be, but we certainly need to know who or what this is, if only as a protection.

As already explained for 1260 years in fulfillment of prophecy the Church of Rome tried to destroy Christianity by removing the Bible, by destroying it's people, causing many to flee as was the case of those who boarded the 'Mayflower' and helped make the United States the 'land of the free.'

Revelation 13: 7 tells that......*the beast (Antichrist) was granted to make war with the saints and overcame them*....that was the Inquisition.

But notice Daniel 7,25which reads....*he will change time and **laws**, and they will be given into his hands for a time, times and half a time.*

Will think to change law.......If you are coming in place of Christ whose laws would you want to change – God's Law.

The Pope has power to change times, to abrogate laws and to dispense with all things, even the precepts of Christ.

Decretal de Translat, Episcop.Cap
The Pope can modify <u>divine law</u>
Promto Bibliotheca, Pope art. 2

The Ten Commandments - King James Version

1.   Thou shalt have no other God's before me
2.   Thou shalt not make any graven images
3.   Thou shalt not take the name of the Lord vain.
4.   Remember the Sabbath day

The Church however, after changing the day of rest from the Jewish Sabbath on the seventh day of the week, made the Fourth Commandment refer to Sunday, the first day of the week as the day to be kept as the 'Lord's Day.'

"Sabbath...A Hebrew word signifying rest....Sunday was a name given by the heathen to the first day of the week because it was the day on which to worship the Sun."

John Eadle, D.D. LLD ...A Bible Encyclopedia, p. 561

' She took the pagan Sunday and made it the Christian Sunday .... And thus the pagan Sunday, dedicated to Balder, became the Christian Sunday, sacred to Jesus.'

Catholic World, March 1894. p 809.

So, who changed it, the Bible or the Church? "Sunday is our mark of authority...The Church is above the Bible and thus transference of Sabbath observance is proof of that fact."

Catholic Record, Sept 1, 1923

Here the Catholic system is saying that if you acknowledge Sunday as the day of worship, you are acknowledging the authority of Rome, you are not only acknowledging her as the supreme power, but you are acknowledging that she is above the Bible ..... and Sabbath transference from Saturday to Sunday is proof of that fact. There is no way you can get around it, it is confirmed in their own documentation.

In the Old Testament Sanctuary or Tabernacle you either faced west, to the ark, to the mercy seat and the Most Holy, the Shekinah Glory of Yaweh.... In (Satan's) system you face the east, which is called an abomination in the sight of God. We see this in Ezekiel 8:16 where 25 men at the entrance to the temple were bowing to the east, to the sun which was an abomination.

Martin Luther recharged them when he came across a Bible and from it found that what he had been taught was not in line with the Bible. This led to the Reformation, Luther 1483 – 1537, followed by Calvin, John Knox and others.

Luther split the angle of error into 95 different concepts and maintained that the Bible was the ultimate authority and that he would do what he had to do to correct matters .

Today the identity of the Antichrist is covered up, but back then they knew and were prepared to die for it.

In 1521 Luther was called to recant before the Church hierarchy he said "I cannot submit my fault either to the Pope or the council, because it is clear as day they have frequently erred and contradicted each other. Unless therefore, I am convinced by the testimony of Scripture...I can and will not retract...Here I stand...I can do no other, So help me God, Amen!"

Directory of the Inquisitors, p 144,148,169 says;

"He who is without the church can neither be reconciled nor saved. He is a heretic; who does not believe what Rome hierarchy teaches – A heretic merits the pains of fire. – By the Gospel, the cannons; civil law and custom, heretics must be burned"

Hundreds of thousands were killed as they stood up to the Roman Catholic Church.

Daniel 7.25 reads.....*And he (the antichrist) shall wear out the saints of the most high...until a time, and times and dividing of times.*

Surely the foregoing would provide the needed courage, incentive and reason for people to heed the warning in Revelation 18 verse 4 where it is written ...*Get out of her my people or share with her in her sins and her plagues.*

9. A CLOSER LOOK INSIDE RELIGION

In all religions there is an Exoteric and an Esoteric sector. Mystical Traditions – Religious Traditions, Gary H.Kah. Those on the outside, the masses and the few who constitute the inner core or circle. It is the same in Secret Societies where only those at the very centre of the organization are fully informed and aware of what is going on.

So it is with the church where the vast majority are sincere, dedicated God fearing people totally unaware about what is going on deep inside the church and there is much evidence to show that this would apply to most churches today!

Today, there are a multitude of Bibles, how does one choose? Wherever the so called 'Counter Revolution' started by the Jesuits gained a foothold, the Vernacular version was suppressed and the Bible kept from the laity. So eager were the Jesuits to destroy the authority of the Bible – the 'Paper Pope' of the Protestant's as they contemptuously called it – that they did not refrain from criticizing it's genuiness and historical value to the law and to the testimony.

Scriptures that help identify the truth were gradually put away or hidden and over 64,000 words have been removed from the modern Bible translations in the past 140 years.

Matthew 24.5 ...*take heed that no man deceives you* - Satan cannot openly get the world to bow down to him so he uses the church as a front, a disguise or cover behind which to operate and it was not long after the last of the Apostles fell asleep in death that his infiltration of the early church began through a combining of Church and State and the beginning of the Holy Roman Empire.

Might this be a wake-call for folk to start seeing and taking seriously what is really going on in the world and also to properly understand and expose the churches involvement which is key in the entire matter? The Bible warned that this would happen. Notice this in 2 Thessalonians 2.2...*The day of the Lord is here. 3. Let no one seduce you....it will not come unless the apostasy comes first and the man of lawlessness gets revealed, the son of destruction.*

He is in opposition and lifts himself up over everyone who is called a God an object of reverence, so that he sits down in the temple of God publicly showing himself to be a God.

The Pope is not only the representative of Jesus Christ, but he is Jesus Christ himself, hidden under the veil of flesh. And God himself is obliged to abide by the Judgments of His priests and whether or not to pardon. Catholic National, 1895.

'Receive the Tiara, be ordained with the triple crown and know thou art the Father of princes and kings, victor of the whole world, replacement of Jesus Christ and receive the glory and honor that has no end and belongs to you. Morgan Thomas, *Pontiff p. 332.*

The church is run in such a way that the laity are not permitted to know anything about what is going on deep inside the church nor are they permitted to read the Bible.

On the face of it the Church is a hugely prestigious organization, immaculate in every respect, spread out around the world with many fine cathedral's and buildings, wonderfully well run and efficient hospitals, schools, universities managed and run by an army of loyal people dedicated to caring for the flock, the 'faithful' and it would be absolutely preposterous to even suggest that this is all part of a cover behind which Satan 'operates,' were it not true and what you are reading is clear evidence of that!

The last place anyone would suspect to find Satan is in the church and yet there he is with all religion under his control.

So again, it should, not come as a surprise to anyone that Satan would be found using both the world's largest Christian Church and the World's greatest nation as covers and vehicle's behind which to operate and achieve his purposes.

Revelation Chapter 13 considered in the previous chapter clearly shows in verse 11 the modern day identity of the Anglo-American world power as the *two horned lamb that would start talking as a dragon (like a devil)...surprise?*

So, you are invited to look further at how the Bible explains how this great deception is being carried out.

In Revelation 13: 3, 4 we were told that ....*all the world wondered after the beast (the Papacy) and they worshipped the dragon (Satan) which gave the power and authority unto the beast.*

Here Satan the Great Dragon is shown in his role as the world's ruler, empowering the Papacy, the church – but we need to take an even closer look to see how it all works;

Satan has a network and God has one;

God's Network; Service to God and Studying his Word, Service to man and Evangelizing His Word.

Satan's Network; Sport, Magazines, Sex, Porn, Music, Parties, drugs, alcohol, tobacco, homosexuality, Spiritualism, Secret Societies, Work, Health.

This is the system we are living in today, setup to so preoccupy us that we will fail to recognize the signs of the times and thus succumb to Satanic deception that will end up destroying us!

Notice 2 Corinthians 4 verse 4…..*the god of this system has blinded the minds of unbelievers that the glorious good news about Christ who is the image of God might not shine through.*

To throw a little more light on what we are up against notice the following extracts of the inscriptions on the 'Emerald tablets of Toth' claimed to date back 36,000 years and alleged to have been found beneath a Mayan temple in Mexico in 1925 and translated by Maurice Doreal;

'Forth come they into this cycle, formless were they, of another vibration, existing unseen to the children of earthmen.'

'Yet beware, the serpent Unseen they walk among the places where the rites have been said; <u>again as time passes, shall they take the semblance of men.</u>'

'Sought they from the kingdom of the shadows, to destroy man and rule in his place-

Also, notice what follows; *"Seek not the kingdom of shadows, for evil will surely appear,* **for only <u>the master of brightness</u> shall conquer the shadow of fear"** *(Jesus?)*

"Know ye, O brother, that fear is an obstacle great; be master of all brightness, the shadow will disappear....heed my wisdom, the voice of LIGHT is near."

Don Jaun, a Mexican Indian shaman, tells Carlos Castaneda the following;

"We have a predator that came from the depths of the cosmos and took over the rule of our lives. Human beings are its prisoners. If we protest, it suppresses our protest. If we act independently, it demands we do not....

"No,no,no,no," [Carlos replies] "this is absurd Don Juan. What you are saying is monstrous. It simply cannot be true." "Why not?" don Juan asks calmly. "Why not?Because it infuriates you?"

"There are no more dreams for man but the dreams of an animal who is being raised to become a piece of meat; trite, conventional, imbecilic."

Being relative few in number the Anunnaki – An, Lucifer or Satan and his demons, these extraterrestrial invaders of the planet need the Illuminati as a front for them to carry out

69

their agenda for the creation of a planetary dictatorship with us humans as a type of micro-chipped robotic mind controlled slave population that will gradually be replaced by hybrids.

These reptilians have been working to regain control of the planet they believe is theirs. Sumerian tablets dating back to around 3500BC tell of the arrival of the Anunnaki who interbred with Earth races to create bloodlines through which to manipulate the world while appearing to be human.

The book of Dzyan tells of a reptilian race it calls Sarpa or Dragons who came from skies to bring civilization to the earth. It's leader was called the Great Dragon. The same was true in China of the Lung Wang or 'Dragon Kings' who were described as part human, part serpent.

Nagas were described as a very advanced race or species and the offspring from the interbreeding of humans with serpent gods. The Nagas intermingled with the 'white-people' to produce a reptilian-mammal hybrid that became.... *The Aryan Kings!* These are the same bloodlines that ruled the Sumerian Empire, Egypt, Babylon, Greece, Rome and today's Anglo-American dual world power!

Indian legend says that the Nagas could take human or reptilian form at will. This is referred to by the UFO,ET fraternity as 'shape-shifting.' Buddha is claimed to have been of the royal line of the Nagas as were the Chinese Emperors.

Satan the Adversary is described in the Hebrew Torah as the 'Old serpent' or Dragon and the ruler of the Nephilim who fled within the earth after losing a cosmic battle for supremacy.

Notice how this is confirmed in the New Testament in the Book of Revelation 12:7....*And war broke out in Heaven, Michael and his angels battled with the dragon and the dragon and its angels battled.*

8. It did not prevail...

9.so down the great dragon was hurled, the original serpent, called Devil and Satan who is misleading the entire earth and his angels were hurled down with him.

We are almost there, either we bring this hidden dictatorship to an end and enter God's Millennium of Peace or God forbid we face a future in a global fascist prison state.

Why would such critically important information not be forthcoming from the Church? Obviously, it would blow apart and undo the guise and cover that Satan has used to mislead and deceive the world.

10. THE INQUISITION AND 'DARK AGE' THINKING

It's [the Jesuit's Order's] objective was, and is still to destroy the effects of the Reformation and <u>to re-establish the Holy Roman Empire</u>.

Throughout its existence the Church has conducted an Inquisition that resulted in the slaughter of huge numbers simply because they were not in agreement with it's teachings when these were not in line with the Bible. Luther found 95 such exceptions.

The Catholic Church is a respecter of conscience and of liberty....Nevertheless when confronted with heresy she has recourse to force, to corporeal punishment, to torture...she lit in Italy the funeral piles of the Inquisition

Alfred Baudrillart 'The Catholic Church Renaissance and Protestantism' p. 182 – 183

Experience tells us that there is no other remedy for evil, but to put heretics (Protestants) to death; for the (Romesh) church proceeded gradually and then tried every remedy. At first she merely excommunicated them; afterwards she added a fine; then she banished them; and finally she was constrained to put them to death.

Cardinal Bellarmine – an estimated 100 million Christians were killed during the middle ages!

So, according to the Church taking a stand for the Bible is evil and warrants Death. How ironic if it were not for the truth about what's going on deep inside the church! Surely, this should not be allowed to continue and yet the Inquisition was never disbanded but continues still, but under the name of the 'Holy Office!

11. QUEEN ELIZABETH l AND THE SPANISH ARMADA

In 1588 Phillip II of Spain sent an Armada to try to subjugate England, but the attempt failed, due in no small part to the tenacious stand taken by Queen Elizabeth l, that comes across in her famous 'Tilbury Speech';

Queen Elizabeth l

Speech to the troops at Tilbury

I know I have the body of a weak and feeble woman; but I have the heart and stomach of a king, and of a king of England too, <u>and think foul scorn that Parma (Italy) or Spain, or any prince of Europe, should dare to invade the borders of my</u> realm;) to which rather than dishonor shall grow by me, I myself will take up arms, I myself will be your general, judge, and rewarder of every one of your virtues in the field. <u>We shall shortly have a famous victory over those enemies of my God, of my kingdom, and my people.</u>

Likely, this great British Queen who stood so firmly against such overwhelming odds would feel totally betrayed if she were to know where Britain stands today in it's support of the E.U. and it's sinister agenda. Brussels being the 'de facto' head of the E.U. and very likely also, the coming New World Order Government under the United Nations!

It would seem that God wanted something better for His people rather than that they should become a province of a Spanish Catholic Empire in some new dark age.

Instead from that time forward Britain went on to become a first rate naval power and in the process established an empire upon which the 'sun would never set.' Her thirteen colonies in North America later would become the New England States and the cornerstone upon which the United States was built.

In fact this also testifies to God faithfully delivering and fulfilling Bible prophecy. In Geneses God made a series of prophecies to Abraham, Isaac, Jacob, Joseph and his two sons Egyptian born sons, Ephraim and Manasseh found in the book of Genesis. Notice one in particular found in Genesis chapter 27 verse 28....*and may the true God give you the dews of the heavens and the fertile soils of the earth and the abundance of grain and new wine. Let peoples serve you and let national groups bow down low to you......Cursed be each one cursing you and blessed be each one blessing you...*

Where in all history has there been a dual nation world power that has possession of the most fertile soils of the earth other than today's Anglo- American world power and its Allies?

What needs to be understood is the fact that the 'birthright' promises which were made unconditionally by God to Israel, were withheld seven Biblical times because of Israel's repeated disobedience. But, were faithfully delivered many decades later to the descendants of ancient Israel referred to in the Bible as the 'lost sheep of the house of Israel,' today's Anglo American peoples spread out across of the earth occupying the most fertile soils of the earth as is undeniably the case with Canada, America, Australia, New Zealand and South Africa.

Notice again, the accuracy of Bible prophecy which comes to the fore showing that from the time of ancient Israel being taken into captivity by Assyria in 721 B.C. until 1800 A.D. when the capital of the United States moved from Philadelphia, Pennsylvania to America's new capital in Washington D.C., would be seven Biblical times according to the Bibles day for a year principle;(7 x 360) would equal 2520 years, viz., 721B.C. until 1800 A.D., would be 2520 years less the zero year.

The following extracts are from my first book 'In God We Trust;'

Does history not testify which people have been the recipients of such vast material blessings? Interestingly the symbols on the British Coat of Arms written in French between the Lion and the Unicorn are, *'Honi soit qui mal y pense'* meaning..."Evil to him who thinks evil" of Britain. Also the inscription, *Dieu et mon droit,* means "God and my birthright."

Likewise of equal interest is the Great Seal of the United States that has numerous sets of 13 on it .The eagle holds in its right claw an olive branch-a symbol of peace, having 13 leaves, 13 berries. In it's left talon the eagle holds 13 arrows, upon it's breast is a shield with 13 bars and 13 stripes and a scroll bearing 13 letters-E Plurbis Unim! Was it co-incidence that the United States began with 13 colonies. Also notice the 13 stars in the 'glory' arranged in the 'Star of David' formation within the cloud that represents the 'in dwelling' glory of God or in Hebrew the 'shekinah.' Strange that Manasseh or modern day America was the 13th tribe of Israel. Was the unseen hand of God somehow involved in all this?

From virtual obscurity at the beginning of the 18th Century Britain - Ephraim and later America -Manasseh emerged on to the world scene to take positions where in a short space of time they together collectively controlled almost three quarters of the most productive land in the world in fulfillment of the Genesis prophecies.

Why would one group of people be put above all the others. This is explained in the Book of Genesis Chapter 12.1 *And God proceeded to tell Abram..."Go out of your country and from your relatives and from the house of your father to the country I shall show you." 2. And I shall make a great nation of you and I shall bless you and make your name great....in you all the families of the earth shall be blessed. It was through Abraham's seed that Jesus would come and through him death the way of Salvation would be opened to all.... John 3;16*

C.H. Spurgeon in *Treasury of the Old Testament wrote..." I judge that God has blessed the two great nations of the Anglo-Saxon race, England and the United States and given them preeminence...(so that) ...they may spread abroad the knowledge of the Glory of God."* Certainly, The Anglo-American people have distributed millions of Bibles in virtually every known language throughout the world.

Notice Psalm 105 verse 42. *For He remembered his holy promise to Abraham. 43 So he brought out his people (from Egypt) with exultation...4. And gradually he gave them the lands of the nations. 45... to the end that they might keep his commandments and observe his laws.*

Notice Exodus 19.5 *If you people will obey my voice you will become a peculiar treasure above all other peoples because the whole earth belongs to me. 6 and you will become to me a kingdom of priests and a holy nation .8. the people answered unanimously "All that Jehovah has spoken we are willing to do." Immediately Moses took back the words of the people to Jehovah."*

Of the struggle of the Anglo-Saxons westward it has been written there could be .....*no grander theme upon the scrolls of history. The very streams of Europe mark their resting places, and the root of their ancient names.*

In a similar vain notice the *'Declaration of Abroath' the 'Scottish Declaration of Independence.'* Drawn up in 1320 A.D. by King Robert the Bruce. This document embodied a Scottish appeal to Pope John XXll on appeal on their behalf to King Edward ll of England to allow the Scots to live in peace.

The Declaration states;......the Scots journeyed from Greater Scythia (Russia) by way of the Pillars of Hercules (Gibraltar) and dwelt for a long while in Spain (Iberia)....Thence came , twelve hundred years after the people of Israel crossed the Red Sea, to their home in the west where they live today. The Declaration reminds the Pope how the Scots received Christianity: 'Nor would He (Christ) have them confirmed in the faith merely by anyone but the most gentile Saint Andrew, the Blessed Peter's brother. Indicating that the Apostle Andrew had followed Jesus' command to ....*Go to the 'Lost Sheep' of the House of Israel.*

Notice Matthew 10.5....*these twelve Jesus sent forth....'do not go off into the road of the nations....6. but instead go continually to the lost sheep of the house of Israel. 23......you will by no means complete the circuit of the cities of Israel until the Son of man arrives.*

Notice also what Jesus said in Matthew 15 verse 24....*I was not sent to any but to the lost sheep of the house of Israel.*

 Later, the Apostle Paul was made the apostle to the nations to bring in people from the nations as brought out in the Book of Romansin chapters 10 and 11.

Unfortunately, however from the very beginning America was plagued by Satanic interference, in that the Constitution forced upon it was a creation of Scottish Rite Freemasonry, similar to the constitutions of the former British colonies.

While most Americans no doubt will have heard about what are referred to as the Federalist Papers, few without being well versed in law, would have any real understanding of what was involved in what has been a long standing attack on the Bill of Rights eroding the powers of both the people and of the States to the end of providing the Federal Government with unlimited and total power to the end of establishing a World Order Government. See 'Our Masonic Constitution' From J B Campbell JBC@wealthkeeper.net Appendix II.

Certainly, this indicates what a firm hold the 'wicked one' has on your Union! What people urgently need to realized and appreciated is that our only real hope is spelt out in John 3.16..... *God so loved the world that He gave His only begotten son that everyone exercising faith in him might not be destroyed but have everlasting life. Jesus said I am the way....*

The absolute importance of this issomething all need to know for there is no Salvation except through Christ, Acts 4;12. There is no other way out of theSatanic deception that entraps not only America, but the whole world!

It is....only through faith and a simple belief in Christ dying for us that will save us, it is a free gift, it cannot be earned! Certainly God knows how to protect His own ...... neither will He leave you, nor forsake them (you!)But know that now is the time to act, as comes across in 2 Peter 2,9......*Jehovah God knows how to deliver people of godly devotion out of trial but to reserve unrighteous people for the day of judgment to be cut off.*

Know also that God is love and that He cares very much for every single one of his human family as our loving Heavenly Father and Creator and our taking in accurate knowledge about Him and His purposes will not be in vain.

Also, know that God will not allow the earth to be ruined beyond repair. Rather it will be those doing the ruining that will be removed and as explained by Jesus in his famous 'sermon on the mount'.....*the meek or righteous will inherit the earth.* Matthew 5 verse 5.

So, that is where we are in the stream of time and certainly God will soon have to act as surely there are limits even to God's patience.

Might this also provide the Creator's answer to global warming and climate change for certainly He is in full control and of this we need have no doubt!

And yes, despite all the excuses, all the arguments raised up against the truth of the Bible, at this late hour it would be wisdom on the part of everyone to puttheseaside and know that what Creation has been groaning for is almost upon us, it is right here .....being indifferent at the very mention of God or the Bible as so many are inclined to be through Satanic propaganda and deception would be foolish as .... you would not want to blow your chance to live in the coming 1000 year Millennium of Peace when the earth will restored to the paradise earthly home that was purposed by God in the beginning for the human family when new scrolls will be opened.

Notice how this is guaranteed in the Bible in Isaiah 55 verse 11......*so shall my word go forth out from my mouth.....it shall not return to me empty but it shall accomplish that which I purpose.* For not one word that God has spoken has failed to come true.

God is a Spirit, we cannot see God that is why He sent His Son, the second most powerful personage in the universe so that as the image of God, we could see what God was like...... yet despite Jesus being a perfect man, the world chose to kill him. God had to restrain himself and watch His own Son suffer an agonizing and torturous death.

So, what this means for any who might refuse the free gift offered by Christ dying for us, would be that they would actually be wronging themselves and would have only themselves to blame if they were to forego their chance of living forever.

A recent documentary entitled 'Privileged Planet' by two Astro biologists shows as never before how truly awesome Creation really is and provides a glimpse of what our kind and loving Creator holds in store of those who pass the final test at the end of the Millennium and go on to everlasting life.

So, It would seem that only those who are willing to accept God's righteous standards will qualify as permanent citizens of the Universe, as clearly God will not allow a repeat of what has happened on planet earth since Eden. Likely if you were in that position, you to would adopt a similar position, so don't let there be any crying that God is not fair ..... He certainly will not force anyone to accept this free gift of salvation. It is a decision that only you can make and show appreciation for by living your life in a way that is pleasing to God and deserving of so great a salvation.

What are God's qualities; love, power, justice and wisdom. He is also a God of loving kindness and mercy, the greatest quality being love and yet His commandments are not burdensome... and are really for our benefit, so it's all aboutus having the right attitude and seeing through Satanic deception that has tried to lay the blame for everything that has gone wrong on God and not himself, for he is the one that is actually been causing all man kinds woes and ills with his *rule or be ruined* form of governance.

Know also that Satan doesn't care what you believe as long as it's not the truth. Might this explain why there are so many different religions and beliefs around the world which is simply that they have confused the simplicity of faith and salvation through Christ's Sacrifice.

Hopefully, this will explain the need for God's Kingdom....which simply is that in days gone by there were kings and kingdoms, just as today there are governors and governments. Yet no government has succeeded in satisfying the needs of all it's people only God's government or Kingdom through Christ will succeed in doing that.

That will be a time when all our present ills and troubles will be forgotten. And yes, this could be just months away, not years as in the past. We are almost there!

Would it be that 2014 was what we have been waiting for? All that we are still waiting for is the fall of 'Babylon the Great,' the confused state of Satan's worldwide system of false religious under the Great Mother Church where all the main line religions have formally acknowledged the Supremacy of the Pope in many instances without the knowledge of their congregations.

It would seem that everywhere great efforts are being made to bring an end to the wars and conflicts around the world and to create and achieve a climate of peace conducive to the establishment of the long overdue World Government. A type of last ditch,' now or never' attempt and effort to make this happen. A bringing together of foes, like North and South Korea, even in a hopelessly war torn Syria where the U.N. is trying to sustain a fragile ceasefire that is hoped will bring about peace.

12. THE ILLUMINATI

Now for a closer look at how Satan runs the world through those under his influence.

The Church is on both sides in any conflict and its role in supporting Hitler and the Nazi's has been quietly swept under the carpet. Might this be one of the reason why history is no longer taught in schools?

What needs to be realized is that Pope is only a front man, a mouth piece for the real power behind the Church, the Jesuit General or 'Black Pope,' who it is that actually runs the world through the Illuminati and the Round Table that encompasses a conglomeration of secret societies and enlightened ones who make up their members.

The most powerful person in the world some might say is the President of the United States, but the truth is that it is the Jesuit General. How do we know that he is more powerful than the Pope? The book by Nino le Bello explains; The Pope's confessor, an ordinary priest must be a Jesuit; he must visit the Vatican once a week at a fixed time and he alone can absolve the Pope of his sins. (more likely to give him his instructions.)

The Vatican Empire, Nino le Bello,

New York ' Trident Press' 1996 p 78.

If you trace Masonry up through all its Orders, till you come to the grand tip-top, head Mason of the World, you will discover that the dread individual and the Chief of the Society of Jesus are one and the same person. (he wears black all the time)'The Black Pope,' M F Cusack, Middleton, Idaho; CHJ Publishing 1999 p.302.

See my lord, from this room I govern not only Paris, but China: not only China, but the whole world, without any one knowing how I manage.

Michael Angelo Tomburini, 1720 General of the Jesuit's Speaking to Duke of Brancan

History of the Jesuit's, Andrew Steinmetz. Philippines, Penn: Lea and Blanchard, 1848Vol 1p107

Notice how President Woodrow Wilson, described this unseen power at work – "Some of the biggest men in the United States in the field of commerce and manufacturing are afraid of something. They know that there is a power somewhere so organized, so subtle, so watchful, so interlocked, so complete, so pervasive that these had better not speak above their breath when they speak in condemnation of it."

Marquis de Lafayette - French Statesman and General who served in the American Continental Army under General George Washington described matters – "It is my opinion that if the liberties of the United States are destroyed, it will be the subtlety of the Roman Catholic Jesuit Priests, for they are the most crafty, dangerous enemies to our religious liberty. They have instigated most of the wars of Europe." And no doubt even the recent conflict in the Ukraine. Who were those ultra rightwing neo-nazi's fascists with their masks, the Maiden activists, with their SS Das Reich emblems and 'Black Sun' occult symbols on their vehicles some who even spoke with American accents? One leader addressing the crowd was heard saying that they "wanted the Europe the Crusaders fought for, a white Europe!"

So that is the Church with its real leader....[the Black Pope] He is the power behind the throne as the real head of the hierarchy. The whole machine is under the strictest rules of military discipline.

U.S. Brig Gen. :- Author of the book: <u>Rome's Responsibility for the Assassination of Abraham Lincoln</u>

<u>Jean Baptiste Janssens 1946 – 1964</u> - <u>Superior General of the Society of Jesuits</u>

<u>Notice the structure of his organization; In Command of:-</u>

- <u>The Order of the Illuminati</u>
- The Sovereign Military Order of Malta
- Scottish – Rite Shriner Freemasonry
- The Knights of Columbus
- The Knights of the Klu Klux Klan
- B'Bai B'nith (Jewish Freemasonry)
- The Nation of Islam and it's private army (called the Fruits of Islam)
- The <u>Mafia</u> Commission
- Opus Dei

R W Thompson

Most believe that the KKK is something belonging to America's past but clearly that is not the case with it'smembers still operating behind the scene. That both Rev Jessie Jackson and now even President Obama are reported to be Princeton Hall Free Mason's which begs the question how could this be so when the KKK is a part of that organization's controlling body, the Church of Rome?

[The Jesuits] are the deadly enemies of civil and religious liberty. Nothing that stands in their way can become so sacred as to escape their vengeance

The truth is, the Jesuits of Rome have perfected Masonry to be their most magnificent and effective tool, accomplishing their purposes against Protestants...

The Grand Design Exposed,

Thomas M Harris – The organization of the (Roman Catholic) hierarchy is a complete military despotism, of which the Pope is the ostensible [is apparent] leader; <u>but of which the Black Pope[Supreme General of the Jesuits] is the real leader</u>. He not only has command of his own order, but directs and controls the general policy of the [Roman Catholic] Church.

The Jesuit Order therefore stands before us as the embodiment of a system which owes it's temporal political domination through temporal political means, embellished by religion, which assigns to the head of the Catholic religion – The Roman Pope – the role of a temporal overlord and under shelter of the Pope – King and using him as an instrument, describes how it will itself attain the dominion over the whole world.

Napoleon Bonaparte

The Jesuits are a Military organization, not a religious order. Their chief is a general of the army, not a mere father of a monastery. And the aim of this organization is power, power in its most despotic exercise – absolute power, universal power, power to control the world by the volition of a single man.

Jesuitism is the most absolute of despotism and at the same time the greatest and most enormous of abuses...

The General of the Jesuits insists on being master, sovereign over sovereign. Wherever the Jesuits are admitted, they will be masters, cost what it may....

George W Malone, U.S. Senator

I believe that if the people of this nation fully understood what Congress has done over the past 49 years, they would move them out of Washington; they would not wait for an election.....It adds up to a preconceived plan to destroy the economic and social independence of the United States. (for details see www Rense.com – the 45 Declarations for the American Communists take over of America.)

Meyer Amschel Rothschild

Allow me to issue and control the money of a nation and I care not who writes the law. (the Rothschilds are the guardians of the Vatican's money.)

The last place anyone would suspect to find Satan is in the church and yet there he is with all religion now under his control. And if the Bible tells this to be so and if the late Pope John Paul ll would actually confirm it, as do other clergy, we had better believe it

The late Pope John Paul II undoubtedly was a humble, honest and God fearing man who will go down in history for his part in bringing down the 'Berlin Wall' that precipitated the collapse of the former Soviet Union. But when history is finally written, perhaps what he said as recorded below will even overshadow his part in the downfall Communism.

"We are now standing in the face of the greatest historical confrontation humanity has gone through. I do not think that wide circles of American Society or wide circles of the Christian community realize fully it. Stop! Read this again! We are now facing the final confrontation between Pope John Paul II, the church and the anti – Church of the Gospel verses the anti – Gospel.

Cardinal Karol Wojtyla (Pope John Paul II)

http:///www.indarticles.com/articles/ml_mOMKY/ls_9_27/al_108881880

Ignoring the second part of his message we need to realize that something is going to happen, something of tremendous importance! Was the Pope trying to sound a warning to American's, in fact toall American's regardless of denomination? If not, why the use of the words 'wide circles of America Society or the Christian Community' in almost cryptic language and why would this be on his personal website and not the Vatican's. Also, why was it not simply addressed to the faithful, his flock?

The great man that he was, undoubtedly knew that something very wrong was going on deep inside the church of which he strongly disapproved and wanted desperately to warn people, all people, especially those in America, hoping that they will wake up before it was too late! Obviously, he could say no more, not wanting to suffer a fate similar to that of Pope Clement XIII who was poisoned on the eve of his announcing the disbandment of the Jesuits.

'Anybody who is acquainted with the state of affairs in the Vatican in the last 35 years is well aware that the prince of darkness has had and still has his accomplices in the court of St. Peter in Rome.'   The Fatima Crusader, Fr. Malachi Martin
"The devil in the Catholic Church is so protected now that he is like an animal protected by the government."
            Cardinal. Milinge cited papal statements to back up his claims.

No doubt Pope John Paul II was only too well aware of the need to 'watch his back' in those quarters, regardless of his high position! He had already survived one attempt on his life

So, clearly what needs to be done is for this to be openly exposed to the world and for America to cease in it's present covert role as law enforcer to Rome and instead do as Napoleon did – close down the entire operation, the huge scam that is being carried out under the cover of religion before it succeeds in destroying us all.

Could the Church not be encouraged to openly confess her sins and grant liberty to it's captive laity, or would that be wishful thinking.......surely that would be in the best interests of all concerned?

In my earlier books it was stressed that the World Government that was supposed to have come into effect soon after 9/11 was fortuitously delayed by the Iraq war lasting 6 years instead of the 6 months that was planned and was further delayed by the collapse of the financial markets from which the world is still trying to recover.

So, we are now in effect in what could be equated to as 'extra time' similar to that allowed in a football match. In other words very likely it is through Divine mercy that we have 'bought time' and 'those days' have or will be cut short.......and all the gruesome tribulation stuff, like all taking the mark of the beast as mentioned in Revelation Chapter 13 verses 16,17 maywellnot happen!

After Armageddon when the wicked are removed, survivors will find themselves in the promised Millennium of 'Peace and Righteousness.' For certainly God is in control and does not need to see more of Satan's wickedness!

Again, as you go through this writing you will likely agree that there is something very wrong with the world that desperately needs to be fixed.

The greatest satisfaction anyone can have in life is to know that one has achieved ones true purpose. This does not necessarily have to come about with fanfare or wide acclaim, it is simply knowing that youhavedone your God given duty in the very best interests of others, in this instance for all humanity.

So, I sincerely ask that you will consider the matter with an open mind and look for ways to assist in getting this information out to family, friends and loved ones and to thinking people in your circle.

Again, Ecumenism is a spurious and crafty device that is being used to bring Protestantism down and to be made subject to Rome with the Jesuits s overjoyed watching Protestantism as they put it, in it's 'death throes.'

Already the mainline churches have been deceived into going along with Ecumenism in the 'let's all get along' way that is put across by acknowledging (in writing) the supremacy of the Pope!

If Satan is to succeed in his efforts to disqualify vast numbers from qualifying for God's Kingdom then clearly the focus in these last days will be on 'swaying' and deceiving the masses.

People are going to be deceived, vast multitudes of them will be deceived into receiving the Mark of the Beast if that happens...give them a copy of this

It doesn't matter what percentage of 'rot' is in the system. What matters is that there is a link between the Antichrist (Papacy) and Satan! What matters is that the dragon (Satan) gives the Antichrist his seat, his power and authority.

Clearly Ecumenism is the greatest threat to Christianity, it puts Christ on the same level as false Gods.

In 2005 the Anti Christ was calling for Ecumenism, a coming together of the world's religion's (including the mainline churches where this has already happened), –to be made a priority – like ancient Babylon, all the world to be made one – but that was Unity in Error - Christ also wanted unity, but unity in truth and love.

In an ecumenical world (the Son of Man had to be removed) so that you can go refer to Krishna, to anyone to save the world. Like we are after-all, waiting for our Cosmic Christ, are we not? Definitely not Jesus!

The UN is leading us to a One World Religion – In the name of World Religion the UN appears to have embraced a sort of religious universalism that views all religions as equals and is seeking to ban proselytizing.

No Christian Bibles are welcome at the UN because you can't be saved by the blood of Jesus. Jesus has to be taken off His throne and put down.

This is not intended to vilify ones church, or religion, but simply to state facts that should not be ignored and go unnoticed. As clearly the whole world has been deceived by Satan. This is something that the American people need to know, if the freedoms and liberties for which America stands are to be preserved!

When the United States rules the World, the Catholic Church will rule the world.

Archbishop Quigley 1903, The Chicago Tribune.

This war is about worship and who it is that must be worshipped. It is a continuation of the war that happened in heaven and is continuing here on earth.

Here the agenda comes to fore – again it's Unity in Error – Protestant's got away from Rome to get away from false doctrine and persecution and for taking a stand for the truth of God's Word, the Bible!

It was upon this foundation that America was built...! Martin Luther found 95 instances where Church doctrine was out of line with the Bible! (Likewise in South Africa the Hugenots were Protestants who fled France, Holland and other countries of Europe and laid the foundations upon which South Africa was built.)

Satan's 'truth' has an 'angle of error,' no matter how good it may sound, if it does not align itself completely with the Word of God, then it is not from God – the gap between what is the truth and what Satan would like it to be. Obviously Satan does not want us to remain in line with the Word of God.

To explain this we can draw an analogy with rat poison which basically is made up of 99.95% good food and only .05% poison – why would they eat it? – the reason's rat's eat it is because it is the 99.95 % good food that they enjoy, they are unaware of the .05% that kills!

The stronghold of the mind is therefore the strategic centre of the war with the god of this system, because it is primarily through the mind that he holds captives in his power. Jesse Pera Lewis. The Battle of the Mind p.4

The Reformers were prepared to die for their beliefs, not today's Protestant leaders and herein lies the danger. At this late hour for the individual, the Bible counsel in Revelation 18.4...is to ' Get out of her. 'To get out of any form of religion that has any signs or traces of the influence of ..... Satan's false system of worship that the Bible calls Babylon the Great.

Also, this is not about running Catholics down, most of whom are good people and were God's people long before ever became Catholics and have no idea of what is going on deep inside the Church. Again Revelation 18 verse 4 carries an urgent warning for them to...... *get out of her (Babylon the Great) my people or share with her in her sins and plagues.*

So, there it is, that is the war that has going on in the world that few know or even care about, a war of deception, a war so sublime so well planned and executed that you don't even know that it is happening and more importantly that you are being deceived and this is being done through both your religion and your political system with Satan and his demons and those under his influence and those who have sold their souls, now operating with impunity from behind the world's Greatest Country and the world's largest (supposedly Christian) religion. That's where he is, having infiltrated and captured both Church and State!

Hence in the Bible Book of Ephesians in chapter 6 verse 12 it is written that..... *'we have a wrestling not against blood and flesh, but against the governments, against the authorities, against the world rulers of this darkness. Against Wicked Spirit Forces In The Heavenly Places.'*

And yes the 'The Four Horsemen of Apocalypse' are now at a full gallop and have been for the past 100 years. Notice in particular; .... *a fiery colored horse and the one seated upon it that was granted to take peace away from the earth.* Revelation 6.8.

13. SATAN AND SATANISM

The Bible tells the end of a matter to help strengthen our faith. So, who is this 'unseen enemy of mankind? He is not Almighty and certainly not invincible, Notice please, the end of this enemy of God and of all mankind found in Isaiah Chapter 14; 12 -17.

"To the Heavens I shall go up. Above the Stars of God I shall lift up my throne...14. I shall make myself resemble the Most High." 15. "However, down to Sheol you will be brought, to the remotest parts of the pit. 16. Those seeing you will gaze even at you; ......saying 'Is this the man that was agitating the earth, that was making kingdoms rock, 17. that made the productive land like a wilderness and overthrew its very cities.....

This is no fictional cartoon character as he is often depicted, the cute two horned character dressed in red with pitch fork in hand, no this is the one who was hurled to the earth with a third of the angels of heaven who are now demon's and <u>he is very active in his role as 'Ruler of the World' as confirmed by Jesus in John 14.30.</u>

As we continue, the word 'occult' has acquired a bad name and we are advised to keep clear of it. But the actual word simply means 'hidden' and the same knowledge can be used for good if used with positive intent.

If used without understanding or with ill intent you can connect with the lower forth dimension. Here the emphasis is on living without fear....fear of death, fear of being alone, fear of poverty, fear of war the list is endless,

The emotion of fear resonates by vibration to the frequency range of the lower fourth dimension below our third dimension. That is why the Illuminati continually create situations, events like wars, designed to keep people in fear of so many kinds. Also the fear or energy we generate can be absorbed by these lower fourth dimension entities and increase their power to recycle it back against us. Fear connects us to them and feeds them energy.

Again Revelation 12 verse 11 reminds us that .....*the great dragon was cast down, the old serpent, he that is called the Devil and Satan, the deceiver of the whole world; he was cast down to Earth and his angels were cast down with him.*

Some researchers suggest that that the reptilians were banished from the earth by the closing of the inter-dimensional portals but that groups with advanced knowledge began to use it malevolently and the portals were reopened allowing these fourth dimension beings to flood back. These portals are to be found in various places across the earth.

In their rituals Satanists summon these demonic entities into their presence by creating the 'vibrational doorways' that allow them to manifest. Human sacrifice, blood drinking and the fear that accompanies it create such vibrations. Such rituals are happening all the time across the earth and some very prominent people are involved. Bohemian Grove in northern California is one such centre for Illuminati ritual the most important being held on 23rd July annually which is attended by top ranking elitist individuals. Another would be Burnham Beeches outside of London in the United Kingdom.

The Church of Satan was founded by Anton LaVey in 1966. His maternal grandmother is said to come from Transylvania, in Romania the legendary home of the bloodsucking vampire Count Dracula. LaVey is claimed to have discovered Marilyn Monroe working in a strip club and used his contacts to make her a movie star.

Hollywood or Hellewood, the sacred wood of the Druid's is awash with Satanists as is the entertainment industry as a whole. LaVey's connections in entertainment and politics included President John.F.Kennedy, Frank Sinatra, Sammy Davis Jnr, Peter Lawford, Jayne Mansfield who was a high priestess.

The Temple of Set was formed in 1975 by Michael Aquino one of the most notorious exponents of the Illuminati's mind control network. Aquino had worked with LaVey in the Church of Satan but broke away to form his own organization that was involved the mind control and torture of men, woman and children. He was also involved in the U.S.Military's Psychological Warfare Division. He was described by a former mind-controlled slave of an elite group called the San Diego Illuminati. He was a cold arrogant, ugly person in heart and spirit, enjoyed using people, had a weakness for young boys and was a confirmed pedophiliac"

Interestingly, the leaders of two 'opposing' terrorist groups in Northern Ireland, the Catholic IRA and the Protestant Paramilitary group the UVF were members of the same Satanic covens which is a classic example of how the

Illuminati operates where again and again it turns out that in 'opposing sides' their leaders turn out to be on the same side in the Illuminati when you get near the top.

Powerful Satanic networks are able to disguise many Satanic related crimes simply because it has infiltrated state bodies, police, the media, the judiciary, political institutions also the churches where top police, politicians, clergy and others are Satanists.This you will find the world over.

Symbols, words, colors, images, sounds and techniques are being used today by the Illuminati controlled media of which the public are not even aware in advertising to hypnotize us to expand the global hypnosis within the human race in the same way that Hitler's Propaganda Minister Joseph Goebbels used slogans and mantras over and over, hypnotizing the mass psyche. Where all alternative views and information were censored and the people programmed to accept inaccurate and biased information! As such Satan continues to deceive the world without anyone knowing.

Satanism and their rituals and sacrifices are vital for the continued reptilian control of the planet. Satanists in pivotal positions ensure that the truth is covered up and the official number of Satanic ritual murders that are happening all over the world are a small fraction of what is really happening. Also the system ensures that those who are not Satanists or their puppets under their control are sifted out before they make it to the top jobs in the institutions that direct society. This is why the ratio of Satanists, blood drinkers and human sacrificers to people in power is so astonishing high compared to the rest of the population.

14. GOD'S SOVEREIGN RIGHT TO RULE AS CREATOR OF THE UNIVERSE

Most folk likely would say that God is ruler of the world. But the Bible says otherwise, notice 1 John 5;19....*We know we originate with God but the whole world is lying in the power of the wicked one.*Otherwise how could Satan have offered Jesus *'All the kingdoms of the world and their glory......If you will fall down and worship me.* Matthew 4 ;8,9

Satan was allowed into this position to address the 'free will' issue he had raised against God's Sovereign Right to Rule as Creator of the Universeto set a precedent that would ensure that never again would God allow his Divine Sovereignty to be challenged.

Satan's challenge to God was that by having free will,man kind should be allowed to rule itself (of course underthe unseen influence of Satan and his demonsfrombehind the scene.) Whereas in Jeremiah 10; 23 it was written that....*that it does not belong to man to even direct his own step.*

So what Creation now awaits is the vindication of God's Sovereignty and right to rule with Satan's form of ruler-ship having shown itself to be an utter failure. Certainly man has dominated man to his own injury.

However, fortunately the battle has already been won by those mentioned in Revelation 12; 11....*they conquered him because of the blood of the Lamb and because of the word of their witnessing and they did not love their souls even in the face of death.*So certainly there would be some who would accept God's Sovereignty and right to rule.

So, clearly what has been raging down throughout history and is still going on actually is a war about worship and who it is that must be worshipped.

As such it should not come as a surprise that Satan would operate from behind the world's religious system that the Bible calls 'Babylon the Great'....Satan's system of false religion with the *wild beast (the Papacy)* as it's leader with all religion now under his control.

Again in all religions there is the esoteric part, the insiders, and the exoteric part, those on the outside who know little about what goes on deep within the organization and are simply being used by Satan to achieve his purposes.

The Bible tells the end of a matter to help strengthen our faith. It has done this by identifying this unseen enemy of mankind and showing how he operates from behind religion. In fact from behind the world's biggest religion and now also from behind the world's most powerful nations, the Anglo American dual world power.

So that's where America is today ..... while the State of the Union may appear to be good and getting better, there are headlines that do not make good reading to mention a few;

.... America is in a perpetual state of war notably with it's *'arc of interest'* and troop deployments encroaching dangerously close to mainland Russia and for that matter also China, despite the assurances given by western powers that when the Iron Curtain came down that there would be no expansion of Nato eastwards. However, Bryzinski and other think tank strategists behind the scene saw the

Ukraine as the ultimate prize that would ensure victory over Russia. It is this that has led up to the present situation!

There is also the humanitarian crisis with more refugees and displaced persons now than at any time in history with as one commentator putting it that the white Caucasian people were responsible for the killing of more people than any other group on earth since 'Regime Change' became official U.S. policy in the early 90's during the Clinton Administration.

Media reports have told that all countries are tired of Western bulling, Western machinations and a slighted propaganda campaign currently focused on making Russia out to be the aggressor when in fact, it is the other way around with America being the real instigator.

........Washington's meddling has turned a dysfunctional state (the Ukraine) into a failed state.

.........the E.U. needs another failed state like it needs a hole in the head - they (the E.U.) already has a long queue of bankrupt existing members not to mention wave after wave of refugees flooding into Europe to escape the destruction of their homes in Africa and the Middle East that can be blamed on the failure of Regime Change operations by Western nations and the resulting chaos!

.........that a showdown with the world's largest nuclear power will achieve - exactly what?

.........'On the Asp of War,' Pope Francis (Huffington Post)

About the last headline what can we take away from this? Clearly, what the Pope is saying is that even if it would mean nuclear war – there will be a New World Order. Not, Putin, nor anyone else is going to change that! This can by no means be taken as an idol threat, it will happen if Church history and the way it goes about achieving it's purposes is anything to go by. Will it take Divine intervention to stop this sheer and utter madness?

15. THE KING OF THE NORTH AND THE KING OF THE SOUTH

In the Bible book of Daniel there are two characters that come across; .... The *king of the north and the king of the south.*

The demise of the Soviet Union in December 1991, presented serious students of the Bible with a dilemma as to who would be the next 'king of the North' for the prophecy in Daniel 11; 40 -45 to be fulfilled.

Notice Daniel 11 verse 40; *In the time of the end the king of the South will engage with him in a pushing, and the king of the North will storm with chariots and with horsemen and with many ships and he will certainly enter into the lands and flood over and pass through.*

While there has been much speculation, until recently it has been impossible to say with any degree of certainty who the next king of the north would be.

However, might the answer lie in what led up to Pope Francis recent historical meeting in Cuba on February 12, 2016 with the head of the Orthodox Church in Cuba to end the 1000 year rift in the Catholic and East Orthodox Churches.

What seems to point in this direction was Russian President Putin missing attending a Group Twenty meeting in Berlin on June 10, 2015 and instead going to Rome to meet with Pope Francis. Also, of significance was that at this time there was also a meeting of the Bilderbergers going on in Austria. Why significant, because the establishment of a

World Order Government has always been high on their agenda. Likewise President Putin's concern very likely was to ensure that Russia would not become subservient to a World Order Government controlled by the west.

The rivalry of the king of the north and south and their ongoing struggle for supremacy has been played out in history since the time of the Hellenistic dynasty.

Among the participants in this unfolding drama to mention a few have included; Syrian King Seleucus I Nicator, Egyptian King Ptolemy Lagus, Syrian Princess and Egyptian Queen Cleopatra I, Roman Emperors Augustus and Tiberius and Palmyrene, Queen Zenobia.

With these kings began a long struggle between "the king of the north and south " that stretches into our time as described in Daniel chapter 11 with their respective identities and nationalities changing through the centuries that would fill volumes.

After the split of the Roman Empire into east and west Frankish King Charles (Charlemagne) became emperor of the new Western Roman Empire in 800 C.E. and according to historians this marked the beginning of the Holy Roman Empire.

Centuries later the Austrian house of Hapsburg obtained and held the remaining parts of the Holy Roman Empire until Napoleon 1 delivered a death blow to the Holy Roman Empire which came to an end in 1870, with Rome becoming capital of Italy, independent of the Vatican.

The following year a Germanic empire began with Wilhelm 1 becoming Caesar, or Kaiser marking the beginning of the modern-day king of the north – Germany.

History shows that Britain took on imperial power in the 17th century after a British-Ottoman alliance forced the French to withdraw from Egypt. In 1882 Egypt became a British dependency and was declared a British protectorate after World War 1 when a Turkish khedive or viceroy was deposed. After America's entering World War 1 on the side of Britain, the Anglo-American world Power began and together they assumed the position of the king of the South.

It was through Kaiser Wilhelm that the German Reich extended it's influence and became an imperial power and later Kaiser Wilhelm ll pursued these colonial goals in Africa and other places and wanting to challenge British supremacy at sea he proceeded to build a powerful navy, second only to Britain.

In order to maintain her supremacy Britain expanded its naval program and negotiated an entente cordiale (cordial of understanding) with France and a similar agreement with Russia, forming a Triple Entente, while Germany formed a Triple Alliance with Austria - Hungry and Italy (all Catholic countries) which in effect divided Europe into two military camps.

On June 28, 1914 the assassination of Austrian Archduke Francis Ferdinand and his wife by a Serbian terrorist was the spark that started World War I.

Assured of German support Austria and Hungry declared war on Serbia with Russia coming to Serbia's aid resulting in

Germany declaring war on Russia. When France gave support to Russia Germany declared war on France and invaded Belgium, whose neutrality was guaranteed by Britain. So Britain declared war on Germany with other countries becoming involved.

It was the sinking of the *Lusitania* off Ireland by a German submarine with the loss of 128 Americans that brought America into the war in 1917 and with Britain augmented by U.S. warships and troops Germany eventually conceded defeat in 1918. Wilhelm II fled into exile in Holland and Germany became a Republic. But the king of the north was not yet finished.

With six million unemployed after the Great Depression conditions were ripe for the rise of Adolf Hitler who became chancellor in 1933 and assumed the presidency of the Nazi Third Reich the following year. That is what has led up to the present situation of the king of the north and the king of the south. The rest is history well known to most..

Might this serve as a 'wake up call' to everyone especially to the peoples of the *king of the south*....who I would refer to as the *'lost sheep of the house of Israel.'*

Again, while it is commonly known that today's Islamic peoples are the descendants of Abraham's son Ishmael, it is not so commonly known or accepted that the descendants of Abraham's other son Isaac and Isaac's son Jacob are the *lost sheep of the house of Israel.* The inheritor's of the *birthright promises.*

Notice a few of these promises; Genesis 22.17 *I will surely multiply your seed like the grains of sand on the sea shore* and your seed will take possession of the gates of his enemies. – like Suez, Gibraltar and others. Genesis 27; 28...*And may the true God give you the dews of the heavens and the fertile soils of the earth.*

Surely, these two promises clearly show that it was the English peoples of the world that inherited the *birthright* promises; ....do these people not enjoy possession of the most fertile soils of the earth and control of strategic gates like Suez, Gibraltar?

But, Psalm 83;4 warns that they would always be in danger and under threat from the nations who have repeatedly said *"come let us efface them from being a nation. That the name of Israel may be remembered no more."*

Notice Isaiah54; 5 *"For your Grand Maker is your husbandly owner. Jehovah of armies being his name; and the Holy One of Israel is your Repurchaser. The God of the whole earth...... 6.For Jehovah called you as if you were a wife left entirely and hurt in spirit, and as a wife of the time of youth who was then rejected.*

7. *"For a little moment I left you entirely,"* but with great mercies I shall collect you together."

10. *For, the mountains may be removed and the very hills may stagger."* But my loving kindness itself will not be removed from you, nor will my covenant of peace itself stagger. Jehovah the One having mercy has said.

61 : 5...."*And strangers will actually stand and shepherd the flocks of your people and the foreigners will be your farmers and your vinedressers*

Jeremiah 30; 11 *"For I am with you."* Is the utterance of Jehovah, *"to save you, but I shall make an extermination among all the nations to which I have scattered you. However, in your case I shall make no extermination. And I shall have to correct you to the proper degree, as I shall by no means leave you unpunished."*

24. *....In the **final part of the days** you people will give consideration to it.*

Notice Matthew 10 ; 5. *These twelve Jesus sent forth, giving them these orders.* "Do not go off into the road of the nations, and do not enter into a Samaritan city." 6. But instead go continually to the lost sheep of the house of Israel. 23..... You will by no means complete the circuit of the cities of Israel until the Son of man arrives.

15; 24 In answer he said :*"I was not sent forth to any but to the lost sheep of the house of Israel."*

Romans 11. 25....*For I do not want you brothers to be ignorant of this sacred secret, in order to be discreet in your own eyes; that* <u>a dulling of sensibilities</u> *has happened in part of Israel until the full number of people of the nations has come in.*

26. *and in this manner all Israel will be saved. Just as it is written:* "The deliverer will come out of Zion and turn ungodly practices from Jacob.27. "And this is the covenant on my part with them, when I take their sins away."

28. *True, with reference to the good news they are enemies for your sakes. But with reference to God's choosing they are beloved for the sake of their forefathers.*

30. For just as you were once disobedient to God but have now been shown mercy because of their disobedience. 31. So also these now have been disobedient with mercy resulting to you. That they themselves also may now be shown mercy. 32. For God has shut them all up in disobedience, that he might show all of them mercy.

33. O the depth of God's riches and wisdom and knowledge. How unsearchable his judgments [are] and past tracing out his ways [are]

But there's a warning in Isaiah 26;10......*Though the wicked one should be shown favor, he simply will not learn righteousness. In the land of straight forwardness {the Millennium} he will act unjustly and will not see the eminence of Jehovah.*

It is paramount that every living soul who survives Armageddon into the Millennium holds this warning very dearly in order to pass the final test mentioned in Revelation 20 verses 7 - 9 at the end of the 1,000 years not to be deceived when Satan is released for a short period of time.

16. IN THE BEGINNING

That great and illustrious British Statesman, Sir Winston Churchill once remarked; *"He must indeed have a blind soul who cannot see that some great purpose and design is being worked out here below."*

So, for any who do not believe that they are being deceived there is the analogy of sleep, that the only time you know that you have been asleep is when you wake up. So it is with deception!

What the world has been involved in is a war about worship and who it is that must be worshiped, a war that has been going on down through time. A war between Almighty God, the Creator of the Universe and a rebel contender, the fallen angel Lucifer (Satan the Devil)

Satan's challenge was not that God was the Almighty Creator of the Universe and had a Sovereign right to rule. No!, it was put more subtly, that mankind by having been created with the dignity of *free will* did not need God's ruler-ship and that mankind was capable of ruling itself and should be allowed to do so, butunderthe influence of Satan and his demon's behind the scene.

Needless to say this has been the cause of untold human misery and suffering with Satan carrying out his own agenda for the world and humanity.

All over the world in every native culture, you will find stories of a great flood and incredible geological upheavals between 11,000 And 5,000 B.C.

It has also been told that before the flood there were ancient civilizations when people lived peaceably under the 'Law of One,' something that science refers to as the 'unified field' theory; that everything is connected and ultimately everything is an expression of the same whole energy or universal life force. Also, that civilization began with positive intent and that it was in harmony with the natural laws of the universe, but was taken over by alien invaders who transferred into a very dark place.

What happened has been described as a free – for – all of the 'Sons of Belial,' who were followers of the Temple of the Sun and who created mayhem and destroyed the peace.

It may come as a surprise that Sun Worship continues even today which will explain why the Church changed the day of worship from the Sabbath to the first day of the week, Sunday.

So, who changed it, the Bible or the Church? "Sunday is our mark of authority...The Church is above the Bible and thus transference of Sabbath observance is proof of that fact."

Catholic Record, Sept 1, 1923

The dominant forces that took over ruler-ship of the earth disregarded the Law of One which was based primarily on the preservation of the earth as a beautiful self sustaining home for humanity. Rather these ones driven by greed and a lust for power placed their faith in technology over spirituality and put their system in operation. Is this not a fitting description of today's world?

It was this that caused the 'One Law' priests to lead migrations of the red race west to the America's and other races east to Africa and beyond seeking to preserve the Law of One in these far off lands.

Zulu historian, story teller Credo Mutwa and one of the only two surviving Sanusi says that the situation for humanity is so precarious that it is more important for them to know what is going on than for him to keep his vows of silence. When the Europeans invaded Africa in Credo's words they milked the minds of the Sharman and then killed them.

Similarly, knowledge of ancient civilizations across the world has also been suppressed. One reason is that it helps to keep in place the false Theory of Evolution which in turn is as the Jesuit's put it, was a way to destroy the Bible without getting rid of it.

After the flood these same dark forces were again at work in the post flood early civilization that began in Sumer [in Nimrod's Babylon] which caused God again to intervene by confusing the languages of the people as explained in the Old Testament.

It has been said that the bloodlines that ruled ancient Egypt are the very same bloodlines that rule the world today. That the European Parliament building in Brussels architecture should befashioned after that of the 'Tower of Bable,' surely testifies to this as do other structures such as the Washington Monument that not commonly known signifies Baal worship, symbolized by the human phallus?

The fact of the matter is that Satan knows that his time as 'ruler of the world' is up, but is determined as ever to win by having the entire world made to bow down to him. In other-words if he cannot have the world and all its glory, no one will, not God and least of all, not us mortals and not even the elite! In effect he is holding the entire world to ransom!

Again, it really is that simple, this is what Satan would like as his 'swan song' to be! He doesn't care what anyone believes just so long as it is not the truth which will account for the abject and almost total moral breakdown of society because if he can disqualify all and everyone from becoming part of God's Kingdom it would automatically make them part of his. Thus the need for everyone to have his mark!

Apart from exposing and closing down false religion our resolve should also be to get environmentalists, climatologists, engineers, scientists and others involved in planning and creating the necessary infrastructure for the 'Law of One' to be put into effect as soon as possible and to put an end to further damage to the biosphere and halt climate change leading to peace and prosperity for all. In need call in the angels to help with the larger issues (although likely this will not be necessary and will happen on it's own accord in the new system now at hand).....like the sealing of any cracks in the ocean floor that some suggest may be the actual cause of the increased ocean temperaturesbehind global warming.

It was Mahatma Ghandi who said that the world could take care of man-kinds needs but not its greed. Can things be turned around, might your answer be ... "Yes they can and yes that is exactly what we are going to make happen!"

It has also been said that the wealth created by America now falls into the hands of just 1% of its people whereas in the seventies most of the wealth was shared by 99% of the people which no doubt has come about as a result of globalization and production being moved south of the border and further afield. This situation is confined not only to America but can be found across the entire world where joblessness and poverty is everywhere on the increase with no solution in sight other than for the elimination of the masses which is something that has also been planned from behind the scenefor the masses and dissenters. Otherwise why all the white unmarked airliners parked on runways around the world?

Thus the need for God's Kingdom or government here on earth to bring relief topeople in man-kinds hopelessly *'failed system.'*May we all look forward to the reality of a restored earth in the coming New Millennium of Peace....a time when the lion will lie down with the lamb when all fear is gone. When people will enjoy satisfying work, happy families, plenty of food, good housing and a time when there will be no more greed, crime, violence, poverty, sickness or death. A hint of this comes across in that well known hymn *Guide Me O Thou Great Jehovah.....'Open now the crystal fountain....whence the healing stream doth flow...'*

Do the world's people not long for the time *when nation will not lift sword against nation and war will be no more* when the reality will be of the tent of God being with mankind and of new scrolls are opened resulting in great blessings and a sure hope for all humanity?

Everywhere it is clearly in evidence that the world has reached a stage where it is going nowhere.... As one writer puts it ..... *the world's economy is stuck in the mud*...with the majority of the world's youth unemployed and with no hope for the future. While behind the scene for our would be masters this does not present a problem as more than likely they do have what in Nazi terminology would be called *the final solution.*

So by taking the initiative many, many could have the opportunity to know and understand how they have been deceived by their spiritual leaders, by those who have not had their best interests at heart, but instead have placed their very souls in Satan's hands.

By being obedient to the call from heaven to "come out of her, Babylon the Great" in Revelation 18.4 these ones can go on to become part of the *'great crowd' that no man can number'* mentioned in Revelation 7.9 who will enter the new millennium of peace now at hand. Again, there is no alternative!

So, might it be a case of out with the old and in with the new? A new 21st century thinking that will rid the world of all the myths and falsehoods perpetuated by our unseen masters and for a positive start to bemade for the restoration of the earth and for it again to become the paradise and self sustaining home for the human family that was purposed in the beginning.

A time when as prophesied ......*the pastures will...keep overflowing and the hills are clothed with joyfulness.....pastures covered with flocks and the valleys*

carpeted with grain....they shout in triumph, yes they sing.
Psalm 65 verses 9 – 13.

So, why not encourage one and all to join those spoken of in Isaiah 2.2...*in the final part of the days ......3.many people will say "Come, let us go up to the.....house of the God of Jacob and he will instruct us in his ways...4. And set matters straight respecting many peoples and they will have to beat their swords into ploughshares and their spears into pruning hooks ...Nation will not lift sword against nation nor will they learn war anymore.*

While it would be pure speculation on my part, I sense that there will be a 'gap' after the fall of 'Babylon the Great' when religion is closed down, before Armageddon when wickedness will be removed and it is during this time that through the Grace of God that those, who have not yet decided can decide on which side to stand in this issue. In other words finally taking God's side or remaining with their heads stuck in the sand, deceived by Satan. However for them there will not be another opportunity.

How glad everyone should be that they may never have to taste death and will simply find themselves in the new Millennium, so again I would urge that you take matters very, very seriously and not delay!

We would do well now to look at God's view of false worship which is brought out at Isaiah 1.13.*'Stop bringing in your valueless offerings. Incense is something detestable to me.' 14. 'Your new moon and your festival seasons my soul has hated. To me they have become a burden,. I have become tired of hearing them.' 15. 'And when you spread out your palms, I hide my eyes from you. Even though you make many prayers, I am not listening, with bloodshed your hands have become filled.' 18.'Come now you people Let Us Set Matters Straight. Though the sins of you people prove to be scarlet And Show A Willingness To Listen, they will be made white just like new.' 19.'If you people the good of the land you will eat.'*

While this, the fifth book in a series I have written over the past 15 years to log/ track events during the last days and now the *'Final Part' of the 'Last Days,'* may not reach publishing stage with matters already seemingto be rapidly reaching a climax and while I shall persist, I'm not sure there will be enough time.

(More about this can be found in my book entitled 'The Coming Global Fascist State' an e-book available on KDP Amazon Kindle.com and also through Lulu Books)

The big message really is that ' *it doesn't have to be this way.'* There is no reason why thinking people need to be held captive any longer by 'dark age' thinking.

17. MASONRY

Freemasonry is the biggest secret society in the world. The worship of reptilians and their dragon queens and the placing of their bloodlines into positions of power, is the secret of secrets held within all the secret societies.

Freemasonry is a compartmentalized pyramid arrangement. At the bottom are the three degrees known as the Blue Degrees above which the vast majority of Freemasons never progress to the 33 Degrees of the Scottish Rite or the 10 Degrees of the York Rite. Yet even at the 33rd Degree you still don't know the real secrets unless you are one of the chosen bloodlines. They feed their chosen bloodline initiates into the unofficial Illuminati degrees where the real action and the real secrets are. So we have a vast network of secret societies with millions of members around the world who think they know what the are involved in, but in truth only a very few have any idea what is going on.

Albert Pike who died in 1891......the Supreme Pontiff of Universal Freemasonry in his book, *Morals and Dogma* written for high degree Freemasons reveals how lower degrees are misled.

'The Blue Degrees are but the outer court or portico of the Temple. Part of the symbols are displayed there to the initiate, but he is intentionally misled by false interpretations. It is not intended that he shall understand them, but it is intended that he shall imagine that he understands them... their true implication is reserved for Adepts, Princes of Masonry.

During a 33 degree Freemason initiation ceremony the oath is taken with every Shriner kneeling and taking the oath before the altar with the Qu'ran on top in the name of

Allah, thus acknowledging this pagan god of vengeance as his own (the God of our Fathers) And in the reduct, he acknowledges Islam, the declared blood – enemy of Christianity as the one true path. (Who seeketh Islam, earnestly seeks true direction.)

When you become a 33 degree Mason you know <u>you worship Lucifer</u>, so can we find any of these in Protestantism? While lower degrees understand the G and compass symbols to mean God in fact its meaning is to do with the Generative principle of the Sun impregnating mother earth and the phallus.

In the Supreme Temple Architects Hall of Honor one finds paintings of President Harry S Trumann 33 degree. Among the other paintings of outstanding American leaders are also high degree (33 degree) Free Masons who are church leaders, who are these people?

- Dr Norman Vincent Peale 33degree - Grand Chaplain of the New York, Knight Templar Shrine.

- Bishop Carl J Saunders 33 degree   -   Bishop of the United Methodist Church (how can you be Head of the Methodist Church and worship Lucifer?)

- Rabbi Seymour Atlas 32 degree   -   KCCH

- Dr James Westerbury 32 degree   -   Ex Director and Editor of Sunday Georgia: Baptist Church

- Rev Louis R Grant   -   District Sup, The United Methodist Church

- Rev.Billy Graham 33 degree   -   World's most popular 'Protestant' Baptist Evangelist

- Dr Robert Schuller 33 degree   -   Pastor of the Chrystal Cathedral and host of 'Hour of Prayer' TV program

- Oral Roberts 33 degree   -   Founder of the Oral Roberts University

- Jesse Jackson 33 degree   -   Price Hall Freemason

Again, The Reformers were prepared to die for their beliefs, not today's Protestant leaders.

The light reveals to us the presence of the Christ comes from Lucifer. He is the light-giver, he is aptly named the 'Morning Star' because it is his light that heralds for man the dawn of a great consciousness.

David Spangler

Director of Planetary Initiation, UN

www.cuttingedge.org/news

The true name of Satan, the cabalists say is Yaweh (God) or a reversal of the tetragrammaton – (written in reverse, upside down, pressed together it spells 'Allah')

When the Mason learns that the key to the warrior and the blood is the proper application of the dynamo of living power, he has learned the mystery of his craft. The seething energies of Lucifer are in his hands and before he may step onward and upward he must prove his ability to properly apply them to the enemy.

Freemasonry is not a revival of ancient mystery religions it is a continuation of them.

The Illuminati have created a pyramid structure throughout society that allows them to operate their global agenda. Every organization today is a pyramid with only a few at the top knowing what the organization is about and what it is trying to achieve.

Major Illuminati symbols are the eye, the triangle or pyramid, the five-pointed star, the obelisk and the dome.

The inauguration of George Washington in 1789 was a Freemasonic ceremony in which he swore the oath of office on a Freemasonic Bible. In January 2001 George W. Bush took the oath using the same Bible as did his father more than a decade earlier.

While it is assumed that America is a free and independent sovereign state the truth is that America has never been free of control from London and that the Federal U.S.Government is a private corporation controlled from Europe. The President of the United States is merely the corporation's temporary chief executive, in the same role as the president of the former Virginia Company formed in 1604 by the British Crown and 'aristocratic' bloodlines to steal North America. An extraordinary story, but true. *The Biggest Secret* David Icke.

After the Great Fire of London in 1666 made way for the building of a New City of London in the knowledge that it was to become a major global centre for the Illuminati. In 1694 William III signed the charter that created the Bank of England and the worlds central banking system emerged with its Illuminati masters dictating policy to bloodline managers around the world like the Rockefellers in the United States, the Bronfman's in Canada and the Oppenheimer's in South Africa with a network of bloodline families around them to control the politics, finance, business, media, military in their particular domain from a central dictated agenda. That provides a glimpse of the 'hidden hand' that controls the people and dictates events on every continent and manipulates the world today!

The Illuminati is an organization within organizations like a cancer and into it all major secret societies feed carefully chosen recruits into positions of power throughout the world. While it may sound bizarre even crazy the Illuminati bloodlines are genetically connected through hybrid DNA as a result of interbreeding of extraterrestrial races and humanity over thousands of years.

The age of the Atlantis proved to be a free for all between the Sons of Belial and the followers of the Temple of the Sun. They disregarded the Law of One and driven by greed and lust for power placed their faith in technology which resulted in the empire expanding rapidly earth-wide. The One temple became ineffective while the Sun Temple flourished and the Sons of Belial prospered. This led to the migration of Law of One followers west to the Americas and East to Africa where they sought to preserve the Law of One.

In that pre- flood period the earth was one solid land mass. This even comes across in the Bible in 2 Peter 3 verse 5...... *this fact escapes their notice, that there were heavens from old and an earth standing compactly out of the water and in the midst of the waterby the word of God.* Again the Bible comes across as true.....so we need to take a look at the earth's early history or what might be described as the Pre-Flood era.

Again, it doesn't have to be this way, know that when good men fail to act, evil triumphs.

18. THE PRE FLOOD ERA AND EARTH'S EARLIER CIVILIZATION

Outside of the Bible there are stories of a flood and earlier civilizations like that of the Mayan people in the Yutican Peninsular in Mexico. This seems to be borne out in biological and geological records during a period from 12,000 to 5,000 according to D.S. Allen and J.B.Delair in their book *The Day The Earth Nearly Died*(Gateway Books, Bath, 1995)

So, while Sumer was not the start of civilized society on the earth it was the most significant one to emerge after the catastrophe destroyed the advanced society or the "Golden Age" that is said to have been in existence forthousands of years.

It has been said that all that we learn and discover has existed before; our inventions and discoveries are but reinventions. The Great Giza Pyramid was 500 feet high and consisted of 6,5 million tons of stone, enough stone to build 30 Empire State buildings, some stones weighing over 400 tons, cut so perfectly that fitted together you could not get piece of paper between them.

In Lebanon are structures thousands of years old which include 3 huge stones known as the Trilithon each weighing more than 800 tons placed 20 feet up in a wall with another stone nearby weighing 1000 tons, the equivalent of three jumbo jets.

In Peru at Tiahuanaco on a site dating 11,000 years ago there are stone blocks weighing 100 tons are connected by metal straps. Also in Peru is the Nazca Lines on the Nazca Plain with fantastic depictions of birds and animals that can be seen from the air from 2000 feet. Also the rock carvings dating back more than 10,000 years found on Marca-Huasi plateau northeast of Lima, Peru with animals not native to Peru like a polar bear, African lion, penguin even a dinosaur.

In the Bermuda Triangle between Bermuda and Florida near Bimini are submerged buildings, wall, roads and stone circles like Stonehedge even what appear to be pyramids.

There is the famous map drawn by Piri Reis, in 1513 that charts the South American coast with great accuracy and part of Antarctica before it was covered with ice two miles thick 7000 years ago. While Antarctica was not officially discovered until Captain Cook in 1773 and was not explored in detail until the 1950s.

A noted author and researcher Colonel James Churchward wrote; *Civilizations have been born and completed and forgotten again and again. There is nothing new under the Sun. All that we learn and discover has existed before.*

Once we know about these advanced civilizations that lasted hundreds of thousands of years and the extraterrestrial involvement our whole view of the world and ourselves will change. So will our understanding of what is happening and who is controlling the world today.

Yet, while these and other amazing structures have featured in books and in television programs in recent years they have done little to debunk the official version of history. The destruction of ancient knowledge all over the world in the name of Christianity was the Illuminati or Temple of the Sun, destroying not only history but the Law of One.'

Today the Atlantean Sun Temple is the Illuminati. Throughout the history of the earth and mankind the white tribes have consistently exhibited their ancestral characteristics and this is key.... they have embraced technology and manipulated spirituality to achieve their own ends and are presently leading humanity towards the New World Order and consciously or unconsciously carrying out the agenda of the Illuminati with little regard for the earth, nature or other species in their generally aggressive, dominating way.

In the 1960s a group of Boeing physicists launched a private study aimed at explain certain anomalies of the Earth and other planets of the solar system that could not be explained by normal physics. What they concluded was that around 5000 B.C. was that Jupiter careered through the solar system throwing the outer planets into disarray explaining their present anomalies of direction, spin and speed. Jupiter crashed into a planet that once orbited between where Mars and Jupiter are today and the debris from this planet is the otherwise unexplained asteroid belt that occupies the space between Mars and Jupiter.

According to Zechariah Sitchin author and translator of the Sumerian tablets, a collision between the moons of a planet they called Nibiru and one orbiting between Jupiter and Mars created the 'Great Band Bracelet' – asteroid belt.

The Boeing physicists went further by explaining that part of Jupiter broke away on impact with another planet and they concluded that this body became what we now call

Venus. After devastating Mars, the "Venus" comet was caught by the gravitational pull of the Earth. It made several orbits causing the tidal waves and flooding that ended the "Golden Age" and hurled vast quantities of ionized ice at the poles. Its momentum then hurled it into its present orbit as "Venus" the planet.

Like the Boeing physicists, two independent scientists, DrC.J. Hyman and C. William Kinsman suggest that the Earth once followed the present orbit of Venus and that Mars was located in the present Earth orbit. While ancient legends say that earth days and years were shorter and people lived longer. There are also legendsthat tell that the earth was enveloped in a cloud that became the rain that caused the great flood.

W.T.Samsel in his study of these ancient societies, *The Atlantis Connection* (Starfire Publishing, Sedona AZ 1998.) suggests that the *war* between the gods in ancient mythology, was over the question of intervention or non intervention in Earth affairs. Samsel says that the kings of the white royal lineage ruled Atlantis and what he called the "Sons of Belial" controlled the Temple of the Sun their religious hierarchy and ritual network. Samsel goes on....*that what developed was a free-for-all for the Sons of Belial and followers of the Temple of the Son who disregarded the Law of One and placed their faith in technology over spirituality and driven by greed and lust for power their empire expanded worldwide to the Americas, Africa, the European countries, the Middle East, India and Tibet. The One Temple became divided and ineffective while the Sun temple flourished and the Sons of Belial prospered. During*

132

that time One Law priests were leading migrations of the red race west to the Americas and east to Africa.

It was during the "Golden Age, during the period of Jared, the father of Enoch, the first of the Patriarchs that the Nefilim, the so-called sons of the gods (Angels of the Lord in other versions) appeared on the scene to "marry" human woman. Today's 'Sons of Jared' organization in the United States have pledged a war on the descendants of the 'Watchers" who as notorious pharaohs, kings and dictators, have throughout history dominated mankind. Their publication, 'The Jared Advocate' condemns the Watchers as being like super-gangsters, a celestial Mafia ruling the world.

No Doubt what they are referring are the *demons* Lucifer's angels and the ones behind the Illuminati agenda for the establishment of a One World Government.

Because there are not many of the reptilian and their purest bloodlines compared with the human population they have been protected from exposure by 'middle-men' they have placed between themselves and humanity and they have had to work hard and manipulate to introduce a structure in which key decisions are made by fewer and fewer people as power is continually centralized and humanity is manipulated to police itself and keep each other in a mental and emotional prison.

The reptilians can be physical beings who live mostly within the earth, physical beings that come from the stars (extraterrestrials) and non physical beings, the real centre of power, which exist on other frequencies and use their hybrid bloodlines to manipulate unseen. The reptilians have worked this scam in many parts of the galaxy and while it sounds utterly bizarre, unfortunately it is not!

La Vegas researcher into the reptilian phenomenon summarizes his conclusions as follows;

' From their underground bases. The reptilian , military ETs (establish) ... a network of human reptilian crossbreed infiltrates within various levels of the surface culture's military, industrial, complexes, government bodies, UFO/paranormal, religious and fraternal (priest) orders etc. These crossbreeds, some unaware of their reptilian genetic 'mind control' instructions, act out their subversive roles as 'reptilian agents' setting the stage for a reptilian-led ET invasion. This likely would be the rounding up of those not willing to accept the 'mark of the beast.' So, for these ones would be a matter of faith in line with ....2 Peter 2.9 *Jehovah knows how to deliver people of godly devotion out of trial , but to reserve unrighteous for the day of judgment to be cut off.*

19. MORE ABOUT THE ANTICHRIST, SUN WORSHIP AND FALSE WORSHIP

"He who is without the church can neither be reconciled nor saved. He is a heretic; who does not believe what Rome hierarchy teaches – A heretic merits the pains of fire. – By the Gospel, the cannons; civil law and custom, heretics must be burned"

In the millions people were killed as they stood up to the Roman Catholic Church.

Daniel 7.25 reads....*And he (the antichrist) shall wear out the saints of the most high...until a time, and times and dividing of times.*

Speaking of the Papacy, <u>John Wesley wrote</u>, He is in an emphatical sense, the Man of Sin, as he increases all manor of sin above measure. And he is too, properly styled the Son of Perdition, as he caused the death of numberless multitudes, both of his opposes and followers....

What is the Methodist's position today?

'Methodists To Confirm Catholic Theology On Justification'

> His Eminence Sunday Mbong, World Methodist Council (WMC) Chairperson.

All religion is involved in sun worship.

In ancient Egypt we have the 'all seeing eye' within the various forms of sun worship, like the papacy holding up the Eucharist symbol which he puts into the mantra symbolizing the sun inside the crescent moon. By holding up this sun symbol the pope is able to get Christian's to bow down to this form of sun worship.

The Pope is the only one to be a world evangelist; he could visit all faiths – Islam and Judaism. <u>He prepared the way for a religious new world order</u>.

BBC Apr 2, 2005

Respect for Religion Urgent

In the current International context the Catholic Church remains committed to encourage peace and understanding between peoples and individuals it is necessary and urgent that religion and their symbols be respected.

The tradition of the Dragon and the Sun is echoed in every part of the world. There was a time when the four points of the world were covered with temples sacred to the Sun and the Dragon: but the cult is now preserved mostly in China and Buddhist countries.

The closer one looks at religion, the more obvious it becomes that the whole world follows the beast, exactly the same things are to be found in them all and all nations have drunk of her wrath.

Again, the call from heaven is ...'Come out of her <u>My People</u>.' Revelation 18: 1 – 5

A Compromised view – that God is not Almighty, is the idea most Christian's have. A logical view - a gap theory which attempts to marry evolution with creation by identifying with the antichrist.

By identifying with the antichrist people get involved in cult doctrines that have the agenda to lead people into various forms of sun worship – the Baalhadad, an ongoing process of renewal –the sun is dying and being reborn, which is the core of the reincarnation view – that every time you die you are said to come back to a higher level.

Who is the Creator of Evolution? According to the Evolutionist it is the Sun.

The Bible says of Jesus - I give light and life. Or you turn to the evolutionists who say it is the sun, which is just another marketing tool used by Lucifer to get agnostics to bow down to him through Sun worship.

The theory that we are somehow evolving to something higher comes from the Jesuits and is displayed on the Vatican's own website.

460. 'For the Son of God became a man so that we might become God....wanting to make us slaves in his divinity, assumed our nature, so that he, made man, might make men gods.

Catechism of the Catholic Church, Part 1 (The Professions of Faith . 2. (The Profession of the Christian's Faith), Chapter 2. http://www.vatican.va/archive/catechism/p122a3p1.htm

This is a fulfillment of the lie in Eden....'no you won't die you will become gods.'

The Antichrist is drawing the whole world into Sun Worship ('Temple of the Sun') – even if the members are not aware of it, this is what Rome is doing.

In the Eucharist when the priest holding a gold solar disk which he places in the monstra that has the crescent moon. This signifies the death of the sun god, the sun dying and being reborn in the womb of the moon. In fact all roads lead to Rome with all religions practicing a form of Sun worship. If you like a type of carry over from the 'Temple of the Sun' in former times. But in this instance time and space does not allow to go further into it.

The implications of Darwin's theory created a deep divide in culture, a conflict of natural verses supernatural order. Not only did it offer an alternate account of the Geneses of life of the Old Testament, but it also gave a sense of moral freedom from the Divine Creator and His Judgment; ....Darwinism, as the collective theories were called, changed the course of man's history forever. Twofold reasons :- If Geneses is not accurate, then what about the rest of the Bible also what about one species being more advanced than another?

The Reformers were prepared to die for their beliefs, not today's Protestant leaders.

When Billy Graham retired, Dr James Dobson filled his place. 'Dobson is unrivalled as an evangelical leader, given Billy Graham's advanced age said Richard Land, President of the 16 million strong Southern Baptist Convention's Ethics and Religion Liturgy Commission.

So it's James Dobson who stepped in to fill the void ....with the 'IHS' on his pulpit, which unknown to most stands for 'Isis, Horus, Set' ....there is no end to the deception, it goes on and on...

What does Billy Graham say about standing up for the truth as a Protestant – let him say it...."there is a difference between fundamentalism and intolerance – I felt that God had called me to love all whether Protestant or Catholic.

So by taking a stand for the Bible was not loving all –that's where the poison comes in. This is where you can identify them by their true colors. You see God loves all by standing on truth, he calls all people into truth and out of error.

See how deceptive it is...work with the Catholics ...we have almost 100% support of Catholic's that was not possible even 20 years ago, we have bishops, archbishops and even the Pope is our friend and we have plans for a couple of events that will probably be world news about our relationship with the Church.

The Jesuits were founded to bring Protestants back to Rome. The high degree Freemasons that were filtered into Protestantism are saying the same things that Billy Graham is saying, that 20 years ago there was almost no interaction with the Catholic Church and today the Pope is our friend and that there are events coming up to show how close we are to the Roman Church –today Protestants are acknowledging Rome as their leader.

These people are getting Christian's involved in liturgy– where does this come from – this comes from Vatican II, the drive to get Protestants involved in liturgy, not only do they get Protestants to not have the true Bible in their hands, but they get the young people to put the Bible down so that they will accept anything that is put in front of them.

Rick Warren 'The Purpose Driven Church'

Time Magazine's : THE MAN WITH THE PURPOSE

What does he stand for – we know that he comes from the Schuller Institute where 33 degree masons infiltrate into Protestantism in order to 'seed' error.

'Today there is a growing interest in the Second Coming, when will it happen?' It is not for you to know the time nor day – when the disciples wanted to talk about prophecy Jesus switched the conversation to evangelism. He wanted them to concentrate on the mission. Speculating on the exact time of Christ's return is futile...only the father knows.

If you want Jesus to come back sooner focus on fulfilling your mission, not figuring out prophecy.

Purpose Driven Life p.285, 286

What does the Bible tell us;

Jesus wept over Jerusalem because they were not aware of the hour of their beinginspected....Prophecy is absolutely essential not only in knowing the time, but getting away from deception.

Both Bill Hybels and Rick Warren have gone so far as to say 'It is critical that we keep in mind a fundamental principle of Christian communication; the audience, (not the message,) is sovereign.... Our message has to be adapted to the needs of the audience.

Marketing the Christ p. 145

Colorado Springs New Press 1988

So it's a 'Man Centered Philosophy: It's people that matter not the message! Figure out what mood you want your sermon to project and then create it! p. 269

We made a strategic decision to stop singing hymns in our seeker services p. 285

Saddleback now has a complete pop/rock orchestra p. 290

Rick Warren – Purpose Driven Church

Use more performed music than congregation singing p. 291

The ground we have in common with unbelievers is not the Bible but our common needs, hurts and interests as human beings. You cannot start with a text. P.295

(So again, notice the deception, it's not the Bible, it is our common needs – put the Bible aside!)

Needs based religion is a most subtle form of pantheism, releasing the god is within. I come to church not to hear the Word of God ...I come to get my needs served/fulfilled...a bank loan from a buddy or some other need.... he says there is an agenda about going to church.

The Bible says the exact opposite – don't worry about what you need - worry about what the Lord wants. We can't change the Word of God to suite ourselves!

Matthew 6: 31 -33....*take no thought about what you are to eat or what you will wear.....*

32....... (for after these things the Gentiles are going) for your Heavenly Father knoweth that ye have need of all these things ...33. Seek first the Kingdom.

What about other Protestant Pastors; Well, let's look at Benny Hinn, look at his website, the suits he wears have the look of Catholicism. He is known to be a Templar - insider of Catholicism – those that spit on the cross.

"Don't say 'I have. Say I Am, I am, I am"

Don't tell me you have Jesus, You are everything he was and everything he shall be

Our Pastor in Christ #2 The Word Made Flesh ....Audiotape, side 2

When he puts his hand up - this comes from Mesmer conducting a magnetic séance. Benny waving his hand over a mesmerized subject!

He is an insider infiltrant. The video shows him saying, "Come on here people let me prove the Lord of Satan" – a slip of the tongue? Also in the video he sends out a curse on the audience to the effect that any who watch and condemn his ministry be cursed!

What about Kenneth Copeland and wife Gloria

'You have a God in you, you are one'

The Force of love, audio tape 1987

'Now Peter said by exceeding great and precious promises you become partakers of the divine class. All right, are we god's? We are a class of gods!

Praise the Lord TV Show Feb 5, 1986

Pantheism subtly covered up.

That Adam was God manifest in the flesh 'God's reason for creating Adam was His desire to reproduce Himself....He did just that. He was not a little like God. He was not almost like God. He was not subordinate to God even. Adam is as much like God as you and I could get, just the same as Jesus...Adam in the Garden of Eden, was God manifest in the flesh. <u>Serpent language</u>

Follow the Faith of Abraham, side1

Kenneth Copeland and the words ..'I AM'

"And I say this with all respect, so that it won't upset you too bad. But I say it anyway! When I read in the Bible where He says I Am, I just smile and say, 'YES, I AM Too!"

These people are insider Freemason's ...this is Insider Pantheism and it's disgusting! The sad part is that their messages are getting to millions and millions of people who believe this stuff!

Believers Voice of Victory, Broadcast July 9, 1987

<u>Kenneth Hagen</u>

Word of Faith Magazine, July 1997. Can you believe that he placed the Masonic Obelisk on the front cover, not that many would understand this to be occult symbolism. (power of the Sun God) What is he up to?

Tulsa, Oklahoma is the headquarters of the Oral Roberts and Kenneth Hagen.

Kenneth Hagen and his wife started the Worldwide Rheemer Church whose symbol or emblem is the crown with the cross in it - look underneath. Hagan is a wealthy, wealthy man. On the DVD series you can watch the spectacle of him getting drunk on the Holy Spirit with Kenneth Copeland. He says," this is the first time we've had a full manifestation of that" –(this is not from God, it's demonic!) Kenneth Hagen Blesses......Kenneth Copeland - ridiculous/pathetic –   Unbelievable things are happening in this church. Satanic salutes, handshakes and other sublime occult symbolism are openly on display. You would however, need to view the DVD's (available from info@Homebase.org) to get the full impact of these goings on within Christianity.

TV Joshua claims– "I was sent to earth to save the world."

     But the Bible says No! Jesus was

20. SATAN'S RIGGED SYSTEM – THE SECULAR WORLD THAT IS RUINING THE EARTH

Can it be denied that there is a huge problem facing the world's freedom loving people with no easy or simple solution in sight, save turning to the one and only source of true wisdom? Proverbs 1.33 explains...*the one listening to me.... will reside in security and be undisturbed from dread of calamity.* But, for most because of stubborn pride, that will only be a last resort. Dare we continue in this way with our leaders knowingly or unknowingly serving or being used by Satan?

Can we continue to ignore our Maker? Surely it would make more sense to at least pause and think again about where we are and ask why? Perhaps a good way to start the process would be by revisiting who God is, although this would be the last thing the world would want us to do. Rarely if ever does He even get a mention in our now almost totally secular world. But, if that were somehow to change, the freedoms that would follow are simply too mind boggling to even imagine.

In your minds eye, picture moths and insects flying around a bright light burning themselves out in a senseless frenzy? Does that not fittingly describe Satan's system, our world today, the phony, rigged system that we find ourselves in, with all its grand illusions, its graft and deceit, designed to control the world's population?

 What is going on is really all about control, the ultimate form of control, a global fascist state.Like lambs we are being led to the slaughter by the imposition of a World order government. The Illuminati and those behind it are seeking to impose their will on humanity at the instigation of the one behind them, who since Eden has been <u>trying to impose his will on all humanity</u> in defiance of God!

There is no aspect of our lives that is not being controlled when the real facts are examined. Even the water we drink is contaminated, anything made from fluoridated water, including beer and soft drinks iseffected. They're not only dumping toxic fluoride into our drinking water, but along with it are fluoride additives containing deadly carcinogenic elements, lead, arsenic and radium. Fluorinated water was first used in Nazi prison camps.

If you are employed in a corporate entity most likely you might find that by some strange coincidence that top management and the Human Resource function have one thing in common, most of the executives might just happen to be Catholic, not that you are supposed to notice this.

Likewise this may also be seen in government, in the police departments, in the court system, in immigration. In fact it is evident across the board. Who has been responsible for opening the 'flood gates' and allowing the masses to flow into the countries of the former 'English speaking' world? In this world nothing happens unless someone wants it to happen! {remember the *'toes of iron and clay not sticking together in Daniel Chapter 2...*

What you are seeing is total and complete control. So great is the deception that even the individuals involved are not aware of what is going on and are simply being used as pawns for it is a fact that few if any of the laity or faithful are aware of what is going on deep inside the church.

While it may be too late to change matters, we need to move away from Satan's false light and away from his false promises, and look up and see the vast expanse of real creation and know that there is a God, a Mighty God of Creation, not this fallen rebellious angel and impostor who cannot create and is so intent upon our destruction and blinding us to the truth about God.

But, by being blessed with *free will*, not until we call upon Him (and this is key), can God and will God act to free us from our present bondage, his hands are tied. We are the ones who must decide whom we wish to serve and above all get out of 'dark age' thinking.

In this war, what needs to be realized is that God is both the source and the supreme example of love. God is love I John 4.8. We have neither seen God nor heard his voice. Yet he invites us to enter into a loving relationship with him. How can we do that? The first step to toward loving anyone is to take in knowledge of that one.

We cannot feel deep affection for someone we do not know. So he has provided his Word, the Bible, so that we can learn about him. He wants us to know everything about him and his creation. He has given us the privilege of prayer...James 4.8 tells us....*Draw close to God and he will draw close to you.*

He is our Heavenly Father who wants only the very best for each one of us. He is patient and kind, merciful, long suffering and good, but that is not the image Satan wants us to have of him. Instead he wants us to see God in the worst possible light, as revengeful, hateful and the cause of our suffering.

We were created in God's image, we were given his just laws and commandments, we were designed to love. He wants us to serve him because we love and desire his righteous way of ruling. Love is essential for the peace and harmony of all creation. We were not designed for a mere three score and ten years, he put eternity in our hearts. Ecclesiastes 3.11. It was through Satan that death entered the world and that is the only thing he wants for us......he has deceived the whole world and it is time for that to stop!

So great was God's love that He was even prepared to offer up his Son so that all might have everlasting life. Is it not reasonable that our perfect Heavenly Father would expect us to show loving appreciation for all he has done for us? But there are limits even to his patience and certainly he will act soon to restore his creation to righteousness and bring an end to *those ruining the earth* Revelation 11.18. He will not allow Satan's world, with it's 'might is right', 'winner takes all,' 'survival of the fittest' system of selfishness, violence and greed to continue a day longer than justice requires.

No matter what may come we can always find solace, comfort and refuge in the book of Psalms; Ps 23, Ps 121, Ps 37. Ps.80.

This information is for freedom loving people everywhere, especially the American people. **Once America 'Get's It' so too will the world and the world will be a better place**. Otherwise, if left it will continue to spiral down into death and destruction.....But your help is needed, please don't keep this vital information to yourself, share it with family and friends and may God Bless your efforts.

Also, what the laity need is to realize and appreciate is that for most, they were part of God's people long before becoming part of the Church. They need to know their roots.

21. A WAR ABOUT WORSHIP

Another very important reason for writing this book is to awaken and rekindle belief in the human spirit, for again 'when good men fail to act, evil triumphs.'

All that it would take to end this sheer and utter insanity is for a few good men to understand what is going on and to stand up and say, "Enough" and take whatever steps necessary to close down his operation, the cover that the church provides. Once exposed for what it really is, the entire charade will be over, for nothing can justify what is going on! However, Satan's gamble is that this will not happen and that few would even dare mention this and as such, that his intimidation tactics will work. Oh, that he may be proved wrong!

May a scripture found in 2 Kings 6:16 provide encouragement for us to stand firm...*Do not be afraid, for there are more with us than who are against us.* Elisha prayed and his servant's eyes were opened to see......*the mountainous region was full of horses and chariots of fire all around...Angelic hosts.* Far greater in number than the Syrian Kings military force and this is true today, God and many myriads of mighty angels are posed and ready to go into action to remove wickedness from the world!

So with that assurance, the first thing we need to do is free ourselves. We need to let go of the fear of what other people think of us for standing up for the truth. We need to free ourselves from being followers and step out of the herd mentality and to stop rushing to stop others from trying to escape the insanity of the present system. When we do that we will cease to be the sheepdogs keeping others in line. We will respect the uniqueness of others and allow them the freedom of thought and expression.

We will lead and others will follow. We will stand up and play our part in changing the world from a prison to a paradise in the knowledge that God helps those who help themselves!

Hopefully, what this book will also accomplish will be, a 'Revival of Faith' and of true Christian Unity and a move away from false religion to bring a resounding shout of Praise to God and His Holy Name, so that He may act to 'lessen or cut short those days,' the days of the coming Great Tribulation and show people that unless they start paying attention that they will be bringing all this tribulation upon themselves!

What people also need to realize, which comes across in Deuteronomy Chapter 28 is that we are now in the time of the Biblical Maledictions or curses and that as recipients of the 'birthright blessings,' that those blessings have come and gone with little or no appreciation. Can it be denied that ever since 9/11 there has been a decided change for the worse in America's fortunes as God removes himself as comes across in Hosea 5.15...*I shall go, I will return to my place until they bear their guilt and they will certainly seek my face! When they are in sore straits, they will seek me!*

The most critical issue facing the American people in this time of moral degeneration and ungodliness, is how to prevent America's God given sovereignty and freedom from being surrendered or exchanged for a Fascist World

Government under the United Nations that will bring great tribulation$ not only to America but the entire world?

Certainly by virtue of it's people having *free will* this is something only they can decide. However, it is likely that the majority would even welcome a World Order Government as a monumental event in world history, unless they can be told the truth and about what is really going on and what lies ahead.

Unfortunately, that is where they are now in Satan's system. But they need to realize that if this is allowed to happen and that if a World Order Government is established, God will have no part in it and will remove himself as indicated in Hosea 5.15 and America will find it's self on it's own without the Divine Hand of Protection and will be totally exposed to Satanic machinations which likely will usher in the Biblical Great Tribulation.. Thus the urgent need for the 'Seek Him Early 'message to get out!

Certainly getting rid of God's people Israel has always been Satan's number one priority. He has tried and failed in two World Wars and is now engaged in 'softening' them up with a literal barrage of satanic propaganda to create a 'freedom from care' attitude designed to take them off guard, before his third and final attempt to bring them down.

Again, notice this in Psalm 83.4...*They have said; "Come and let us efface them from being a nation. That the name of Israel may be remembered no more."*

22. GOD'S PEOPLE ISRAEL

The very first instruction Jesus gave his disciples was ...to *go continually to the lost sheep of the house of Israel....*Matthew 10.6., indicating the importance Jesus ascribed to this.

In Geneses 22.17 it was foretold that Jacob's descendents would be......*multiplied like the stars of the heavens and grains on the seashore* and according to Geneses 27.28. they would be given the ...*choicest and most fertile parts of the earth...*(not a mere strip of land along the coast of Palestine occupied by today's modern state of Israel!)

 A short version of the story about the 'lost tribes of Israel' would be that after the collapse of the Assyrian Empire around 612 B.C. the Northern ten tribe kingdom of Israel disappeared into history and became known as the 'ten lost tribes of Israel.'

What is not known about them and has somehow become obscured by history or kept hidden is that they gradually migrated into and across Europe in two great waves. In the first wave they were known to historians as the Cimmerians – or Celts and later, in a second wave they were known as the Scythian or Sacae tribes (sons of Sac – Isaac.)

Also, there would be a withholding period of seven Biblical times (2520 years) from the time of their Assyrian captivity around 721 B.C.. With incredible suddenness both Britain and America or more specifically the dual thirteenth tribes of Ephraim and Manasseh (sons of Israel's youngest and favorite son Joseph – see Geneses Chapter 48 also 1 Chronicles 5.1 and 2 which clearly states that .... **right of first born was given to the sons of Joseph**. (Again this is

Scriptureis a key to Bible understanding that seems to have been missed by Bible students) would suddenly emerge on to the world scene as the Anglo-American dual world power and would be recipients of the 'birthright promises' of unprecedented national wealth and power.

Interestingly, 2520 years later in 1800 A.D. the Federal Government moved from Philadelphia, Pennsylvania to the new Capital of the United States in Washington D.C. Certainly the other tribes were also blessed, but not to the same extent as Ephraim and Manasseh, again a brief account of this can be found in Genesis chapter 49.

 It might also be pointed out that many of today's Catholics were part of Israel long before they ever were Catholics. So again this would provide an example of Satan's 'divide and rule' tactics at work. Looking on, he puts us against one another – showing how absolutely diabolical he and his kind really are! Thus the call to heed the Bible's command to "Come out of her."

Notice Isaiah 45.19...*In a dark place...I spoke not; nor said I to the seed of Jacob, "Seek me simply for nothing.' 49. "You are my servant, O' Israel, you the one in whom I shall show my beauty."*

Deuteronomy 28.2 ...*If you are careful to do all I am commanding you....your God will put you high above all other nations.*

11. You will overflow with prosperity....

Notice Psalm 104 verse 42....*For he remembered his holy promise to his servant Abraham. 43. So he brought out his*

people (from Egypt) with exultation. Notice God's purpose;
44. And gradually he gave them the lands of the nations...(the
choicest and most fertile parts of the earth- unprecedented
blessings of wealth and power Deut 28 1-15)

45. To the end that they might keep his regulations and
observe his laws.

Notice Exodus 19.5...*if you will strictly obey my voice and*
keep my covenants, then you will certainly become a special
property, because the whole earth belongs to me.

6. You will become a kingdom of priests and a holy nation.

8. After that the people answered unanimously ..."All that
God has spoken we are willing to do." Thus they became
God's Chosen People!

KeyTo Understanding God's Purpose For His People Israel
(For us today)Is That;

God wanted His Chosen people Israel to become a nation of
righteous, God fearing people who would be a living
example to people of all nations, showing that God's way's
are infinitely better than Satan's and to help free them (the
nations) from the chains of Satan's dismal prison with all it's
violence and strife, poverty and greed, to the end that all
people would learn and benefit from following God's
righteous ways.

But because of Israel's failure,(and later our failure) Paul
was tasked with these responsibilities and made an Apostle
to the Nations. God ...*turned his attention to the people of*
the nations to take out a people for his name - a spiritual
Israel .Acts 15.14.

But this did not in any way undo God's irrevocable covenant with Abraham and his seed according to their generations to time indefinite. Genesis 17.7

Might it be said that God has always been welcomed into the trenches, but is soon forgotten once peace and prosperity return and after World War II, that is exactly what happened!

Instead of becoming a living example to the world of a righteous, God fearing people there was a gradual spiraling down and a lowering of standards in America and countries of the former Allies, which provided the wicked one with the opportunity he needed to bring about our destruction-we have played right into his hands......that is where we are today!

This trend also found it's way into the Protestant churches, where they dropped or relaxed their guard and failed to cherish their Protestant roots and heritage, providing the 'wicked one' with the opportunity to take advantage of the situation and to strengthen the hand of Rome in order to achieve his own purposes.

Since the Reformation, Protestantism, despite having the Bible gradually became divided into thousands of different sects and denominations each with its own particular version of the truth, whereas the Roman Catholic Church apart from the Eastern Orthodox Church has remained intact. Might it be that divided (we,) Protestants have fallen?

In Deuteronomy 31.29 Moses warned....."*For I well know that after my death ...you will certainly turn aside from the way I* *have commanded you; **and calamity will be bound to befall you at the close of the days** because you will do what is bad in the eyes of your God so as to offend him by the works of your hands."* Like America acting as 'law enforcer' for the Roman Catholic Church and the United Nations. That's where America is today, far removed from what God's purpose was for America being blessed!

At the moment America is a democracy - the government is however, leaning more and more to becoming fascist. This is clearly in evidence in U.S. foreign policy where it's 'Regime Change Agenda' and attempts to enforce 'democracy' has resulted in the creation of more refugees and suffering than in anytime in history.

For all intents and purposes it could be said that America is now very much a Catholic country.

> Revelation 13:12....*he exercises all the power of the first beast before him and causeth the earth and they which dwell thereon to worship the beast whose deadly wound was healed.* It will drive the entire world to bow down to the first beast (the papacy.)It is through the church that worship is directed to Satan.

By following Antichrist (the Papacy) we are automatically channeling worship to the Dragon (Satan). This has gradually been gaining momentum and unknown to most it is being done through Ecumenism, the whole world is now being made to bow to Rome in order that worship may be channeled to the dragon. Not only have the mainline Christian Churches in one way or another acknowledged the primacy of the Pope, but so too have the other world religions evidenced by gathering at the Vatican. Satan needs this in order for the entire world to bow down to Him to prove the challenge he made against God's Sovereignty and right to rule in Eden. But this will be to no avail as according to the Bible in Revelation 12.11 the battle has already been won by those unsung hero's who did not 'love their souls' even in the face of death, but he will nevertheless persist with his agenda until he is stopped.

Notice who God blames for the poor spiritual condition of His people;

25.34...'Howl you shepherd's ... you majestic ones of the flock, because your days for slaughtering and for scattering have been fulfilled.

Again, blame for the poor spiritual condition of the people laid at the feet of the spiritual leaders who have not taught their followers the truth about the Bible and have acted contrary to the counsel given in James 4.4...'Friendship with the world is enmity with God!

Once the truth is presented, honest hearted ones will not find difficulty in understanding. Jesus said in John 10.27...'My sheep will listen to my voice, I know my sheep and they will follow me.'

Obviously, there is so much more to the great deception being carried out in the name of religion to deceive the world ...... but, if anything....know the truth and may the truth set you free and know that God is love and wants only the best for us all so do not allow the 'wicked one' to blind you to the truth.

HISTORY AGREES:

Notice a little about your roots, the roots of 'you the people;'

Of the *identity* of the Sacae and the Scythians who called their country Sacasena and were known to the Persians as the great tribe of Scythians (wanderers) bordering them there is no doubt. It is equally clear that the Saxons of England were the Scythians or Celt-Scythians. Historians all seem to trace the Saxons (Son's of Sac - Isaac) back to the very place where the captive ten tribes of Israel were deported by Shalmannasar, King of Assyria.

In this regard notice the Bible in 2 Kings 17:6 ......*kept them dwelling in Halol and Harbar at the river Gayon and in the cities of the Medes(Persia- now Iran)*. Also, 2Kings 12:23...*God removed Israel from his sight*.

To this testimony historians seem to agree;

Strabo asserts that most ancient Greek historians knew the Saccae as a people who lived beyond the Caspian Sea.

Diodorus says: "The Sacae sprung from a people in Media who obtained a vast and glorious empire."

Ptolemy finds the Saxons in a race of Scythians, called Sakai, who came from Media.

Pliny says: "the Sakai were among the most distinguished people of Scythia. Who settled in Armenia and were called Sacae-Sani."

Albinus says: "The Saxons were descended from the ancient Sacae of Asia."

Prideaux finds the Cimbrians came from between the Black and Euxine (Caspian) seas, and that with them came the Angli.

Sharon Turner, the great Saxon historian, says: "the Saxons were a Scythian nation, and were called Saca, Sachi, Sacki, and Sach-sen."

Gawler, in "Our Scythian Ancestors", says: "The word 'Sacae,' is fairly and without straining the imagination, translatable as Isaacites." (Sons of Sac, Isaac?)

Roman historian Josephus mentions these as the great peoples occupying northern Mesopotamia beyond the Euphrates. Later as these two groups migrated in a north westerly direction across Europe they became known to historians as the Saxon and Celtic peoples.

Notice also the **Behistan Rock Inscriptions** (Western.Iran) by Darius the Great, in the *Persian language* lists Scythia as the 19th province of his empire, while in the *Babylonian language* the same province is called **the land of the Cimmerians indicating that the Scythians and the Cimmerians were in fact the same people.**

 One might ask, "Do the prophets prophesy falsely?" For clearly Jeremiah 33:17 states' ...'*David shall never want for a man to sit on the throne of the house of Israel' (not the house of Judah).* Some may contend, how could this be Israel as never since its exile, has Israel had a throne, nor has any descendant of David ever been acknowledged as its prince? Might what follows unveil not only the modern day identity of Israel but also show how both History and the Bible are undeniably in accord on this issue.

162

Fortunately the genealogical tables have not been utterly lost with the compilation of a list of the royal line from David and Zedekiah to Queen Victoria using very ancient manuscripts in the Herald's College, London. Anderson's 'Royal Genealogies', London 1732. Keating's History of Ireland -Dublin 1733. Lavoisne's Genealogical and Historical Atlas - London 1814 and other such references.

Also, Amos 9. 9 reads......'*For, look! I am commanding, and I will jiggle the house of Israel among the nations, just as one jiggles the sieve, so that not a pebble falls to the earth.*

Thus God purposed his people to migrate across Europe and down through the centuries to emerge on to the world scene in our day, not as the modern day State of Israel no, but rather as The Great Nation and Company of Nations mentioned in Genesis 35.10 who are in fact Great Britain and the United States of America. And as such are the inheritors of the *Birthright Promises* recorded in Genesis 48 and Deuteronomy 28.

23. THE WORLD'S GREATEST SCAM

It would seem that the leadership and elite of the entire world have been corrupted into thinking that somehow they will be the Masters and the rest of us slaves or mind controlled robots in the coming World Order government or dictatorship and that they have bought into with all the Satanic lies and deception, not realizing that in the process, unbeknown even to themselves that they to are being deceived and are simply being used by him to achieve his purposes, which is the destruction of humanity of which they are a part! He is the Arch Deceiver?

But what also seems to escape these ones is that the world's first religion was 'Narcissism' and that it was Satan who introduced it, his 'I Am' philosophy, that us mortals somehow are god's or evolving into a godhead that is freely expounded in our centers of higher education. It is this that he has used so successfully to deceive so many and to deny the very existence of Almighty God! Again, should he be trusted? What guarantees have been secured for surrendering the sovereignty of the United States?

Certainly the Bible tells that there definitely will be a world government, but shows that America and its great resources will only being used to put it in place, after which it's rulership will pass to .... *ten kings who have not yet received a kingdom...Revelation 17.11-13.* How can this not be seen as perhaps the World's Greatest Deception or Scam? [But, if those days were to be 'lessened' none of the above might even be necessary. Does that not provide us the hope, the chance that we so desperately need?]

Beyond the call for a New World Religion, a 'Cosmic Christ' and all the other New Age 'think,' when all is said and done, what this is really all about comes across in <u>Psalm 83.4</u>...'*Let us efface them from being a nation, that the name of Israel may be remembered no more.*'

That has always been the wicked ones goal. Satan will not relent until that has happened, <u>that is what this is all about!</u>[But, again if those days were to be 'lessened' none of the above would even happen. Again, does that not provide us the hope, the chance that we so desperately need?]

Now with God in the process of removing himself as comes across in Hosea 5.15 and with the Great Tribulation and the Maledictions straight ahead. **We of our own volition, will soon find ourselves completely on our own and totally exposed, without that Divine Hand of Protection, in an increasingly dangerous world!** [But, again, for sake of repetition 'if those days can be lessened, cut short' does that not provide us the hope, the chance that we so desperately need?]

Going back to the warning that Islam would grow restless, this is indeed a warning that needs to be taken very seriously when seen against the world's present geopolitical landscape with Isis and radical Islam.

Satan knows that once God has removed himself that he will be free to bring in his bands to finally destroy God's people.

24. A WORLD ORDER GOVERNMENT

The idea of a World Order should be relegated back to what it was, just the 'pipe dreams' and good intentions of some 'good old boys' of yester year...Morgan, Macy, Rockefeller and all the others not to mention Cecil Rhodes, the Rothchild's and is totally 'out of whack' with the geopolitical realities of today's rapidly changing world order!

Even in his time Churchill recognized this.....'*The United Nations Organization was still very young, but already it was clear that its defects might prove grave enough to vitiate the purpose for which it was created.*' So, we most certainly have been warned.

Alasdair MacIntyre said...."the religion of the English ...is that there is no god, and it is wise to pray to him from time to time." So at least they will know where to go when the going gets tough!

O that you British people might revisit the 'Tilbury Speech' and the words of that beloved and brave queen, Elizabeth I, who spoke from the heart and see again who you are, your roots and how far you have come and realize who it was that made the' *winds blow*'. A thanksgiving service was held in St. Paul's Cathedral for the deliverance of the country and a medal struck with the words *"God blew and they were scattered."*

The Queen's confidence in God and her people was rewarded. It was this that made it possible for you to avoid becoming subjects of Phillip II of Spain and the Spanish Catholic Empire and instead to go on to become the world's greatest Nation, the Biblical 'Chief of the Nations' (Jeremiah

31.7) and become a great naval power with an Empire upon which the sun would never set and to spread abroad the knowledge and truth of Almighty God! The defeat of the Spanish Armada also allowed for the establishment of the thirteen colonies, the corner stone upon which the United States of America was built!

God's promise to Abraham [of both spiritual and material blessings] was that "in you all the families of the earth shall be blessed."

How was this tremendous wealth and power? To bring its enemies into submission? No, through the generosity and character of their people's, Europe was rebuilt through the Marshall Plan and likewise the Japan was reconstructed allowing both Germany and Japan to become global economic powers.

James Morris in his work *PaxBritannica* wrote..'It was not merely the right of the British to rule, so the imperialists thought, it was their duty. They were called.' They would distribute across the earth their own methods, principles and liberal traditions that the future of mankind would be reshaped. Justice would be established, miseries relieved.

At the end of World war II, the United States was to become the most powerful nation on earth in the *'Rise and Fall of Great Powers' by Paul Kennedy* we read:' America alone, held the secret of the atomic bomb. It also held two-thirds of the world's gold reserves, half its manufacturing production capacity and half its ships and supplied one third of the globe's exports.'

So come on America and you British cousins, clearly it's time to sort this matter out. This is not

aboutcreating panic, wild hysteria, doom and gloom, but rather a time for cool heads to accept the realities and truth of the situation and to work towards resolving the matter in a calm and rationale way. This should be a call to both the American people and the British peoples to see again the need to jealously guard your *Freedom and Liberties* in an increasingly dangerous world. **A world that has consistently sought to destroy you and your very existence and where your survival has only been possible thru the Divine hand of Providence which you are now in the process of casting aside in exchange for a World Order government under the Church of Rome and the United Nations that will provide Satan, Lucifer, the world dictatorship he seeks! Surely, this is obvious!**

This is also a call to the American people to jealously guard their *Freedom and Liberty* and to understand the need to properly secure America's Sovereignty by safe- guarding the Bill of Rights, in the knowledge that the federalism created by the U.S. Constitution is flawed and is identical to the federalism of the Grand Lodge system of Masonic government and not the supposed friend of the people but rather their controller.

A perfect example would be when John Marshall the first Chief Justice revealed the Mason's contempt for the people in his denunciation of "Judicial review," which simply meant that the Supreme Court was the true power. Where are the checks and balance on the Supreme Court? This becomes particularly clear when considering the make up of the Courts present membership! Extracts taken from 'Our Masonic Constitution'....www.rensecom

Also, notwithstanding this, '*We the people*' - people of the individual states need to be reminded of our (their) power to embrace the 'states rights' under the Constitution and <u>to send to Congress only those who truly understand and support the rights of the people they represent!</u> Those with the necessary resolve and tenacity to work towards the repeal of treaties and agreements that do not truly represent the will of the people that have resulted in millions of jobs being shipped abroad and have brought America closer to a World Government. NAFTA, GATT and all the others. Also, that these elected representatives will work to ensure that the sovereignty and security of individual States are in no way compromised.

Again, how many people realize that the United Nations is actually a provisional entity and that after the Second World War if a peace treaty between Germany and the Allies (which as yet still has not been signed), had been signed, that the UN Charter or mandate would legally have ended?

How many people know that the present German government is in fact illegitimate? The reason the German people are not even aware of this is, despite having Drivers Licences, Passports and other documents purportedly issued by a Second Reich Government, is because the illegal government in Berlin is worried about publicity and being exposed and another reason is because the controlled media is silent on the matter!

Until there is a peace treaty, Germany will technically remain a colony of the United States. After the Supreme Headquarters Allied Expeditionary Forces , (SHAEF) accepted Germany's declaration of defeat, it was quick to recognize the legitimacy of the Zweite Deutsche Reich (The Second German Reich) which was claimed to have been illegally displaced by Hitler's Third Reich!

Only when a legitimate government is established and voted for by the people, will Germany have a legitimate government and the present illegal German government will have to stand down. Following the collapse of the East German Democratic Republic, a treaty confirmed that only The Second German Reich, now led by Reichskanzler (Chancellor) Dr. Wolfgang Gerhard Guenter Ebel, represented the legitimate German State, but that is as far as matters went and the 'illegal' government of the Federal Republic of Germany is still very much in power and the real reason for this is not hard to find knowing the precarious legal position of the cherished United Nation's Organization, upon which the hopes of the 'One Worlder's rests! Might this explain the urgent need for the World Order Government to be put in place?

Interestingly, the first law Proclamation No.1, making U.S.General Dwight D. Eisenhower, supreme authority in areas under U.S.Control was signed on Feb.13, 1944 and these SHAEF laws were to remain in effect for a period of 60 years from date of signing and would apply to all of Europe. This poses the question, what has happened since the laws expired in 2004, if anything? information courtesy – wwwRense.com '**Germany still in Jurisdictional Limbo' and lately being used as a crutch to help support the European Union's failed financial system!** How ironic that the Brussels is the unofficial leader of the New World Order Government with it's European Parliament building actually fashioned after the Biblical 'Tower of Babel.' It is also home to Nato that commands the world's most powerful army and home to the world governments super computer with whose knows what data stashed away in it!

Is it not time 'WE THE PEOPLE' demand that Germany be released from her present bondage?

26. 'COMMANDERS OF ISRAEL'

Notice a timely warning by the prophet Micah ...."*hear, please you heads of Jacob and you Commanders of Israel. Is it not your business to know justice? 2. You haters of good, lovers of badness........ 3. You the ones who have eaten the organisms of <u>my people</u>...smashed to pieces their bones. 4. At that time you will call to your God for aid, but he will not answer...he will conceal his face from you at that time.....*

So, might now not be the time to seriously rethink the entire World Order issue before it is too late? For certainly Satan has deceived the world. Also, our war is not against *flesh and blood but against...wicked spirit forces* Ephesians 6.12

Notice Roman's Chapter 11 which covers the Apostle Paul becoming an apostle to the nations which brings out God's ultimate plan for both Israel and the nations. Notice verse 25... *I do not want you to be ignorant of this sacred secret...that a dulling of senses has happened on the part of Israel until the full number of people of the nations has come in. 26. In this manner all Israel will be saved....32. For God has shut them (Israel and the nations) up altogether in disobedience, **that he might show all mercy**. 33. O the depth of God's riches and wisdom and knowledge....how unsearchable his judgments....To him be glory forever.*

Also, this should not be a time for church bashing, or castigating those deceived individuals (those who have allowed themselves to become possessed by demons) who are helping to put a world government in place. Certainly an individual should be free to decide for himself who to serve and whether or not to heed the call to 'Come out of her,'

Babylon (Satan's worldwide system of false religion) Is that not the American way? There is no need for squabbling about who is right or wrong. Instead should our efforts not be focused more on attaining to the next level, the Promised Millennium of Peace! Do we need to linger a moment longer in this Satanic 'hell hole' that is our present system is becoming and not move on to real life, of real peace, freedom and being the people we were meant to be, this is not a dream, this is for real and deep down this is what every American knows and wants! That is just who you are and if this message can be properly and effectively communicated, likely it would meet with resounding support and prove to be what America and the world have been waiting for. This has to make sense, this is about survival, that is the big message, the alternatives are simply too horrific to imagine and all that is required to turn things around is a little humility and a whole lot of guts. But it would not be the first time in history that the American people have been in a corner!

So, while this book attempts to expose and show how the world has and is still being deceived by the Satanic infiltration of religion, this should not be taken as a personal attack on anyone. While God loves you as an individual, He may hate the particular system of worship you find yourself in, if your religion is not truly in line with His Word. Also, any Catholic's reading this need to know that you were one of God's people long before ever becoming one of the 'faithful.'

27. 'YOU PETER' ..... A SATANIC DECEPTION

THAT SATAN HAS USED BIBLICAL INFORMATION TO
PROJECT LIES INTO THE WORLD IS UNFORTUNATELY A SAD
REALITY. BY PEOPLE (THE LAITY) NOT BEING ALLOWED TO
HAVE A BIBLE AND BY SERMONS BEING GIVEN IN LATIN,
THEY WOULD BECOME VICTIMS OF A GREAT DECEPTION;

In Mark 16. 13 – 19 Jesus asks....*Who do you men say the Son
of man is 14. Some say John the Baptist, Elias, ...one of the
prophets. 15. But what do you say I am? 16. Peter answered
...you are the Christ, Son of the living God. 17. Jesus answered
, blessed art thou...flesh and blood did not reveal this to you,
but my Father which is in heaven, did. 18. I say unto you that
thou art Peter and <u>upon this rock I will build my church</u> and
the gates of hell shall not prevail against it.*

A 'Rock' in the Bible usually refers to a mountain, or a large
stone and is found 119 times as such and everytime when it
refers to a person, it is used to refer either to God or to
Christ. **In this instance Christ would be the 'rock'. He
was the stone the builders rejected, not Peter!**

However, notice the following:-.......' *Thou art Peter [Petros
– a (piece) of rock, stone or pebble] and upon this Rock [
Petra a (mass of) rock] I will build my church.*Pope Benedict
XVI constantly reaffirmed that Jesus made St Peter the
Rock!

The task of giving an authentic interpretation of the Word
of God whether in it's written form or in the form of
Tradition, has been entrusted to the living teaching office
of the Church alone.

Catechism of the Catholic Church # 85

Mark 16:18. *And so I tell you Peter you are a rock, and on this rock foundation I will build my church. - Good News Bible.*

The three metaphors to which Jesus takes recourse are very clear in themselves;

1.   Peter will be the rock foundation upon which the building of the church will be based.
2.   He will have the keys of the Kingdom of Heaven to open and to close to whom he thinks it is just.
3.   Finally, he will be able to bind and to loose.

> For all times, Peter must be the custodian of the communion with Christ.....
> Peter the Rock, Vatican City June 7, 2006.

This is not actually Biblical – that is what is put over to the people, but this beast speaks out of both sides of the mouth.....

'Not a single Father can find any hint of a Petrine office in the great Biblical texts that refer to Peter.' <u>Peters supremacy and infallibility so central to the Catholic Church today, are simply not mentioned.</u>

Not a single creed, nor confession, nor catechism, nor passage in patriotic writings contains one syllable about the pope, still less about faith and doctrine being decreed by him.   ' Vicars of Christ' De Rosa, p. 206

The entire deception hangs on Mark 16:18 and to this Revelation 17:9 says.....*and Satan deceiveth the whole world.....*

This is a shocking revelation...... "I cannot soften it. I was deceived my entire life until someone had the guts to tell me what the Bible actually says." Again, this is a shocking revelation but please understand that God loves every person, but hates the deception, just like when we speak about Christ and the churches from Ephesus to Laodicea when he said he hated the practices of Nicolaus .

Revelation 18: verse 4 says....'*come out of her my people' so that you will not receive part of her plagues...* notice Revelation 17.16 *.......the ten horns you saw and the wild beast, these will hate the harlot and will make her devastated and naked and will...completely burn her with fire*.... This is a call where Jesus loves you as an individual, but hates the system that you might find yourself in!

Many scriptures can be found in the Bible that clearly show that Jesus would be the 'rock' or cornerstone upon which the church would be built.

In Matthew 21.42....*Jesus said to them."Did you ever read in the Scriptures. The stone that the builders rejected is the one that has become the chief cornerstone! "*

Notice also 1 Peter 2.6 where this is confirmed by Peter himself;.....*For it is contained in scripture; "Look! I am laying in Zion a stone , chosen, a foundation cornerstone, precious and no one exercising faith in it will by any means come to disappointment,"* While in Daniel 2.45 we read...'*a stone (Jesus)not cut by hands ' 44. 'will crush and put an end to all these kingdoms.'*

28. 'A HAPPY ENDING?' IT WILL HAPPEN

With the final curtain about to go up on the end of Satan's wicked system and with the promised 'Millennium of Peace' ahead, would it not be wisdom on the part of <u>all you fathers (also all you mothers) to know that it is your God given duty to help your families,</u> your children, your grandchildren to know and understand what is going on, what is about to happen, <u>so that they will not to be deceived into receiving the Mark of the Beast</u>...and will know what to do to survive into the New Millennium. This comes across in Deuteronomy 5 – 25. *'Listen, O Israel...6. These words I am commanding you today, must prove to be in your heart...7. And <u>you must inculcate them in your son </u>and speak of them when you sit in your house. 12 watch out that you do not forget the Lord who brought you out of the land of Egypt out of the land of slaves. 25 it will mean righteous ....*

Surely, for men of goodwill it is time to boldly warn of the grave dangers that lie ahead for the peoples of the once Anglo American free world and to courageously take a stand for truth and righteousness and with the help of Almighty God, assist in setting matters straight in the world's two great democracies!

While fear inspiring times may lie ahead, it is God's Will that you and your families will all enter the Millennium of Peace.

Might it be that there is will be a happy ending to this great saga, like always happens in the movies? Why not? You can make this happen! <u>Make it your business to share the 'Seek Him Early Message' Hosea 5:15 with family, friends and</u>

loved ones as this is the answer to all American AND the world's problems.

Do your utmost to keep the Commandments of God which were given for our benefit and to have strong faith in the Salvation Jesus has offered and thus be marked for life! And above all, be obedient to the call from Heaven to; 'Come out of Her!' And yes, let the world know that we all stand for unity, unity in truth and peace and that according to His Word there will be a peaceful new world in the coming millennium.

Again, notice Revelation 12.11....*they conquered him because of the blood of the Lamb and because of the word of their witnessing and they did not love their souls even in the face of death.* This tells us that the battle has already been won, so that a lessening of those days is now a real possibility and the reason for us to start paying urgent attention and to prepare ourselves for what may be **a sudden and unexpected return of Jesus as 'King of Kings and Lord of Lords' and His mighty angels who will remove the wicked and restore righteous to the world....our eyes will merely see it**! We are rapidly approaching this final part of history. Is that not in itself a good reason for a 'Revival of Faith?'

So, join those spoken of in Isaiah chapter 2.2....*And it must occur in the final part of the days ...7. many will come and say "Come, you people and let us go up to the ...House of the God of Jacob and He will instruct us in His Way. He will set matters straight respecting many people. And they will have to beat their swords into plough shears and their spears into pruning hooks and* *they will learn war no more!" For the former things have passed away...Revelation 21.1*

Revelation 21.4 tells that .....*And he will wipe out every tear from their eyes, and death will be no more, nor mourning, nor pain. The former things will have passed away.*

Notice what is recorded at Roman's 11.25,26.....*I do not want you to be ignorant of this sacred secret that there has been a dulling of sensibility on the part of Israel until the full number of the people of the nations have come in. 26.In this way all Israel will be saved. As it is written, **the Deliverer** will come out of Zion and will remove ungodliness from Jacob.27. And this will be My Covenant with them when I shall take away their sins.32. For God has consigned all men to disobedience that He may have mercy on them all [alike.]* This tells us that there will be a happy ending for all mankind in the coming New Millennium. Read about this in your own Bible, in fact read the entire Chapter 11 of the Book of Romans for a better understanding.

29. OTHER VIEWS

Well known British Author, David Icke in his book, Children of the Matrix has a different take on what is going on in the world, from an entirely non-religious perspective which I shall attempt to para-phrase; (but either way the choice we have remains the same)

What <u>Creation</u> does so magnificently is put the consequences of our choices, in front of our faces, This imperfect world is a consequence of human choice, the choice of those who wish to control and the choices of those that sit back and let them do it, or close their minds to what is happening because they think it is easier that way.

So creation is presenting the consequences of our action or inaction and it is this that makes the world we live in absolutely perfect because we are experiencing what we need to experience. Two apparent opposites, but both are true.

In reality, it is all just a game. A cosmic game called evolution, <u>a game called love.</u>

In this game the longer we stay in denial, the more powerful and challenging the consequences will become. People are hurting, economies are down and until this situation is addressed and turned around, the suffering will continue.

That is our choice. The question is how extreme must the consequences become, before we act?

"We are not humans on a spiritual journey. We are spiritual beings on a human journey. **Stephen Covey.**

So, either way America is at cross-roads and 'We the People' need to make a choice, to do nothing and stay in denial or to stand up and say 'No' to the global fascist state and it's sponsors who are foisting it upon us, regardless of the consequences. What has happened to the saying that...'these colors don't run?

The following are a series of books written over more than a decade warning about what is coming down the line by the author (Robert M. Wettergreen) currently available on www.Amazon.com;

'In God We Trust' Published in 2000...... *warning the American people that something would trigger America's 'roller coaster ride' down to the Biblical Great Tribulation followed by Armageddon. Sadly, a year later the events of 9/11 proved to be that 'trigger.'*

'A Rush To War' published 2010........*written for both the British and American people that tells how some good may have come by the War in Iraq becoming protracted and warning the British people of the need to preserve their God given sovereignty by shedding light on what is described as the World's Greatest Scam.'*

'God's Final Call' A tribute to Mark Woodman published 2011 (some extracts of which you have been reading)......*tells of a war of deception that is moving into it's final phase and explains how our leaders, our elite, even our churches have put a padlock on any mention of this, when in fact even they have fallen into a trap and have got it all wrong and are taking us down a slippery slope of no return that if not stopped will result in billions of lives being lost. Even a* *warning given by the late Pope John Paul II seems to have been ignored .....this is truly news breaking, must read stuff....*

 Sadly, Mark died at the early age of 34 years after struggling with cancer. Any who have watched his DVD's that are available on info@homebase.org will know what an incredible speaker he was!

To become a '*Friend and Lover of Freedom,*' no formalities, you simply make it your business to be one and share the truth with family and friends.

'The Coming Global Fascist World Order Government.' Available from the following websites; www.Lulu.com/Justdone.co.za

These books are also available as e-book on Amazon Kindle.com

Sincerely,

Robert M.Wettergreen

Finally A Simple Analogy On How To Understand the message of the Bible And Religion.

The effects of a divorce putting it mildly, in many instances can be terrible. By way of an example imagine a single mom bringing up a son, doing her best to take care of all his needs. While the father who is a real 'rotter,' offers no support. But the boy loves the father because he's the fun guy, buys him toys, sweets, all the good stuff..

The boy loves his mother, but his dad is his real friend and because of his dad's influence he doesn't think about all the needs his mother takes care of!

Isn't that' really how it is 'here below,' with Jehovah God, like the boy's mother being the one supplying all the needs of the human family, both materially and spiritually.

While, Satan who like the 'rotter' in the illustration, gives us nothing that we really need, but as the 'fun guy' keeps us like moths senselessly flying around a light, burning themselves out in the process.

2 Corinthians 4;4 put's it this way; *he has blinded the minds of unbelievers.* He's like the father – he blinds minds with false promises that the good news of God's Kingdom will not shine through.

The mother for her part does her very best to bring the boy up to become a good moral citizen.

Everyday we are in the world under Satan's influence and as mature Christian's we realize that Jehovah God is our provider. So we have to make a decision who it is we will follow. Notice James 4;4 ....*whoever ...wants to be a friend of the world is constituting himself as an enemy of God.* Like in the illustration - one of the characters will influence the child.

The boy may see through the father – but he likes being with him, even if he knows what the father is all about and gradually he may even become like the father until the mother says "pack your bags and go."

Satan appeals to our desire for pleasure and all that money can buy to win our favor. Ephesians 4;19 puts it this way....'*having lost all moral sense they gave themselves over indulge in every kind of loose conduct with a continual lust for more* – until any relationship we may have had with our God and Creator gets less and less ....*works of the flesh......Galatians 5; 19-20 (provides a long list of such)* The Bible says that the people who practice these things will not inherit God's Kingdom.

People in the world don't even know about the Kingdom, they want everything now, they want to be rich and famous.... They even imitate their role models – want to look and dress like them without considering that such things come with a price and may cost them their eternity if they don't turn around before it is too late!

1 John 5;19....*we know we are children of God, but the whole world is under the control of the 'wicked one.'* It is he that is responsible for all the world's present ills and woes. But the world is passing away and so are it's desires. – yet we don't want Jehovah's way – not realizing that '*he that does the will of God remains forever*' 1 John 2;17. We cannot be friends of both, God and the world.

Even if you make a gross mistakes – don't reject Jehovah God – don't let Satan ensnare you. King David, made mistakes but because in his heart his love was for Jehovah he received forgiveness.

1 John 4.9....*By this the love of God was made manifest in our case Because God sent forth his only begotten son into the world that we might gain life through him.* Being created in his image, he first loved us – we can be Jehovah's friend. Ask

yourself who really is my friend, Jehovah or is it the world? We cannot have both, we have to reject the world to gain the eternity that was put into our hearts. Notice Ecclesiastes 3; 11...*even time indefinite he has put into their heart that mankind may never find out the work that the [true] God has made....*

HITLER A PERFECT EXAMPLE OF AN ILLUMINATI OPERATIVE IN ACTION

Let's pause and see how these ones operate and take a fresh look at recent history and at Hitler who undoubtedly was one of the world's most notorious characters and look at the forces that brought him to power. These are very brief extracts from 'Children of the Matrix' by David Icke.

There is no better example of how Illuminati bloodlines possessed by demonic entities than that of Adolf Hitler. It is believed that Hitler was actually of the Rothschild bloodline. The Illuminati produce many offspring out of wedlock and place them into positions of power.

Austrian Chancellor Dolfuss found from official registration cards of house servants that an innocent young servant girl with the surname that happened to be Hitler had fallen pregnant while working for Salomon Mayer Rothschild, in Vienna. He had a lecherous passion for young girls and there were instances when his adventures had to be hushed up by the police. The story continues but the gist of it is that this child was Adolf Hitler.

When standing on a public on a public platform with that contorted face and crazed delivery, he was channeling 'reptilian demonic' consciousness and transmitting this vibration to vast crowds. 'One cannot help thinking of him as a medium.' For most of the time, mediums are ordinary, insignificant people. Suddenly, they are endowed with what seems to be supernatural powers, which set them apart from the rest of humanity. Hitler was possessed by forces outside of himself. He appeared to live in perpetual fear of "supermen."

Hitler once said to an aide; "What will the social order of the future be like? Comrade I will tell you. There will be a class of overlords......he goes on recounting the hierarchy, the conquered until at the top he mentions an exalted nobility of whom he cannot speak; The new man is living among us now! He is here. I have seen the man. He is intrepid and cruel. I was afraid of him."

Hitler was a member of both the Thule and Vril Secret Societies and spent a lot of time in Barvaria whence the Illuminati had sprung. A big influence on Hitler was the Bulwer-Lytton's novel *The Coming Race.* This is about an enormous civilization inside the earth well ahead of our own. These underground supermen would according to Bulwer-Lytton's novel emerge on the surface one day and take control of the world. The theme of underground supermen or "Hidden Masters" can be found in most secret societies legends around the world.

Dietrict Eckart, a heavy drinker and drug taking writer met Hitler in 1919 and decided he was the 'one,' the Messiah he was looking for. It was Eckart who was credited with Hitler's advanced esoteric knowledge and black magic rituals that plugged him so completely into the demonic reptilians. From now on, Hitler's power to attract support grew rapidly Eckart wrote to a friend in 1923.

Also of note is that the Nazis did not disappear in 1945, they just went underground. The inner core of the Nazi secret society network was the Black Order which continues today and is reported to be the innermost circle of the CIA. Allen Dulles the first head of the CIA was a key force behind Operation Paperclip that protected Nazis like Joseph

Mengele after the war and took them to America. The Dulles family were cousins of the Rockefellers (bloodline in other words), Reinhard Gehlen the man appointed by Dulles to set up the CIA network in Europe, was one of Hitler's SS chiefs. Only Nazis considered expendable were sent to the Nuremberg show trials designed to cover up what happened.

The original swastika, an ancient Sun symbol was right-handed, which in esoteric terms , means light and creation, the positive. The Nazis reversed this to symbolize the left-hand path – black magic and destruction.

So, here the King of the North mentioned in the Prophecy of Daniel Chapter 11 it would seem is alive and well. Does this mean that God's people are without hope and will soon be at the mercy of the dark forces that are behind the coming UN World Government?

At this late hour these ones would be wise to do whatever necessary to hold on to their countries God given Sovereignty's and above all to "Seek Him Early" Hosea 5.15 and trust that the hand of Providence that has never failed them, will again be there for His people in their time of need!

If you are one who would be upset by graphic details and descriptions about what is going on behind the scene you may be a little apprehensive about viewing the information that follows that may be a little too sensitive to your liking. However, by the same token you could regard it as educational. So prepare yourself to take a brief look behind the scene into the 4th dimension from where the unseen ruler of the world and his cohorts op

THE 4TH DIMENSION

To help understand a little about the dynamics of such inter-dimensional covert control we need to understand that we are in the third dimension and they operate from the fourth, a frequency just outside the range of our physical senses. (sight, sound, touch, taste and smell.) You might think of it as a kind of parallel universe.

Like radio waves that we cannot see and are all around us, that can pass through windows and walls, so too can these entities that share our space and can move in and out of our dimension at will.

Einstein tells us that matter is merely energy condensed to a slow state of vibration. Our minds observe the visible and physical world and only what we perceive becomes our reality, and not in fact what really is!

In the Bible there are several references to indicate that Satan and his demon's would be in our midst, notably;

John 14.30 where Jesus says....."*the ruler of the world is coming, And he has no hold on me.*"

Revelation 12.7...*And war broke out in heaven; Michael and his angels battled with the dragon, and the dragon and his angels battled but it did not prevail.....*

9. So down the great dragon was hurled, the original serpent, the one called Devil and Satan, who is misleading the entire inhabited earth, and his angels were hurled down with him. 12. On this account be glad you heavens....Woe to the earth and for the sea, because the Devil has come down to you, having great anger, knowing he has a short period of time.

2 Peter 2.4...*God did not hold back from punishing the angels that sinned....by throwing them into Tattarus, delivered them to pits of dense darkness to be reserved for judgement....*

Job 1.6....*God said to Satan: "Where do you come from?" Satan Answered..."from roving about the earth and walking about on it."* So, he (Satan) is right in our midst.

Also, notice Ephesians 6.12 ...*we have a wrestling not against blood and flesh, but against governments and authorities, against the rulers of this darkness, against wicked spirit forces......*

We are not alone! While we may think we live in our own world or universe, it is confirmed in Scripture that the world is actually being controlled for millenniums by the unseen 'wicked creature' Satan and is demons and also his earthly agents. Those 'possessed' who do his bidding.

In former times and right down through history they operated openly through kings and emperors through the ;Divine Right of Kings.' Today, they do not openly manifest themselves, rather it is done covertly through a network of secret societies that collectively make up a pyramid type structure with the Illuminati at is top, which is run by some of the most famous and well known people on the planet.

Being relatively few in number the Anunnaki (An, Lucifer or Satan and his demons) the extraterrestrial invaders of the planet need the Church and the Illuminati as a front for them to carryout their agenda for the creation of a planetary dictatorship with us humans as a type of micro-chipped robotic mind controlled slave population.

This would account for reports of their bizarre genetic experiments in hidden facilities, one described or known as 'nightmare hall' on Level Six at the Dulce underground base in New Mexico. (The following information was published in LIFO magazine by Researcher Bill Hamilton and TAL Levesque, also known as Jason Bishop lll.)

Inside Dulce there are Genetic Labs, reports by workers tell of seeing bizarre multi-legged "humans" or half human, half octopus. Also, reptilian humans and a vast range of humanoid creatures half-human, half lizard, winged humanoids, grotesque bat like creatures, furry reptilian creatures with human hands that cry like babies. (One worker said)...."I frequently encountered humans in cages usually half dazed or drugged, but sometimes they cried and begged for help. "We were told they were hopelessly insane and in high-risk drug tests to cure insanity. We were told never to try to speak to them."

According to Phil Schneider the son of a German U-boat commander in the Second World War, he knew of 131 underground military bases, an average of one mile deep in the United States, constructed for the New World Order Agenda financed by what is called the 'Black Budget!

Schneider was told that under the new Denver International Airport, east of Denver, there are several main levels underneath, at least ten sub-levels, a 4.5 square mile underground city, and an 88.5 square mile underground base. The Denver base is said to include massive 'containment camps' for holding 'dissidents.' Workers who experienced the deeper levels of the base saw scenes so terrifying they refused to talk about them. From other sources these bases are where millions of children who go missing every year world-wide are taken. They are used for slave labor and eaten by the reptilians, just like humans eat chicken or cattle.

Might this indicate and confirm the desperation on the part of the reptilians to transform themselves into humans perhaps to escape God's wrath? Or vice-versa. There has to be a reason for it. Also for their need to consume vast amounts of blood to sustain their hormone levels and to keep their DNA codes open in order to maintain human form.

To help understand these ones we know that until the eight week the human fetus goes thru many stages of development similar to non human species before taking it's evolutionary path as a human. At one stage the embryo develops gills, even a caudal appendage or tail.

So too in the development of the human brain is the development of a reptilian component, the 'R-complex. It is from this ancient reptilian part of the human brain that we get our cold-blooded character traits. Characteristics such as 'territoriality' (this is mine, get out) aggression; and the idea that 'might is right, winner takes all.' These are the very attitudes of the Illuminati.

Scientists say that the R-Complex represents a core of the nervous system and originates from a 'mammal-like reptile' that was once found all over the world in the Triassic period (250-240 million years ago.)

Fortunately, unlike in reptiles this part of the human brain is balanced by other parts, so we are not completely cold-blooded or unfeeling. There is so much more about the reptilian species that could be discussed that would fill volumes.

Albert Einstein gave us his theory E=MC² showing that matter is a form of energy and that energy cannot be destroyed, only changed into another state. Matter is just energy condensed to a slow state of vibration. X-Ray technology is simply a tuning device that tunes into frequencies that match our bone structure or in the case of say a building can show the reinforcing steel frame by tuning into that frequency.

It is a basic scientific fact that energy cannot be destroyed, but can change form by changing the temperature (frequency) as in the case of ice where ice becomes water and water steam.

Modern technology can show the human aura, even our thoughts and emotions (frequencies) are a mass of different colors (frequencies) that change as our thoughts and emotions change.

So, our very consciousness, is energy and is indestructible, but sadly modern day science and medicine has not advanced beyond this point. While scientists know that 90% of the mass of existence within the atom that is referred to as 'dark matter' is not subject to the laws of gravity and those of the electromagnetic field they have not progressed further by taking the laws of physics that apply to our known frequencies and on this basis judge what is possible in other frequencies.

The term 'dark matter' refers to only what does not reflect light in our frequency range and cannot be seen. The question that really needs to be considered is 'does everything reflect light.'

So we continue to live in this our own dimension limited to what our five senses perceive as reality. Our minds observe only the visible, physical world and in the process allow the enemy to use this to their advantage and they will continue doing so until our appreciation of reality and 'what really is' changes.

We are more than our physical bodies. Plato said that all bodies are only shadows of true reality. Modern or 'Conventional' medicine is purely reactionary and concentrates on the symptoms and ignores the causes that can cause the disharmony or physical diseases.

The point is that we are certainly more than our bodies. We are part of an infinite energy, we are all energy.

There is so much more to this, even the divisions between us are illusions. If we loved each other, there would be no conflict in the world. Neither would the Illuminati be able to manipulate us to look outside ourselves for answers that they know we will never find.

That is why we follow them like sheep believing that the solutions they offer like new laws and powers even the World coming together as One under a UN World Government will work when in fact it will only succeed in destroying us!

Thus the need to look to a higher source of power for the answers we need and for power to change both our inner and outer – selves and attitudes with love, God is love! We were created in His image, to mirror and reflect His love in our lives, only then will our reality become the reality that we are struggling to find!

Credo Mutwa believes that the reptilians originated on this planet and were driven off before returning to claim what they believe is rightfully theirs.

To any who find the idea of a reptilian race to be unimaginable Carl Sagan is quoted as saying, "There are more potential combinations of DNA {physical forms} than there are atoms in the universe."Far from it being impossible for such a race to emerge, it would be more surprising if it had not."

In medicine it has been said that in the United States doctors are now statistically more dangerous than guns. We have a situation where people are actually in hospitals because of the effects of drugs that are supposed to make them well! In the London Daily Mail it was reported that where the cause of death is a hospital acquired infection this is kept hidden from patient's families and are not mentioned on the death certificate! Also, the so called "super-bugs" have mutated immunity to many antibiotics because doctors have been prescribing them like confetti for so long – another behind the scene Illuminati plan to destroy the effectiveness of the human immune system in obedience to their unseen masters. Surely, it is time for change?

It is also said that Science is now a fascist club in which all members must stay in line. So too is it with the medical profession. The whole 'scientific system' is structured to suppress knowledge because the Illuminati is desperate for us to remain in ignorance of who we are and the true nature of life and who we really are! If enough people knew the truth, (what you are now reading) their game would be up!

So, how about you professionals who may now be retired, who may have known about what has been going on during careers, but had to bite your bottom lip rather than expose this evil to preserve your lively-hoods and for the sake of your loved ones to perhaps share your experiences and tell it like it really is. Why not even band together with former colleagues and have your stories told?

Can you honestly say that this is really the world you want to leave to your children, if not why not try to make a difference by doing whatever you can to help turn the situation around?

Know that the Millennium of Peace and Righteousnes will soon be at hand and also the Justice demands that there are even limits to God's patience, know that He will soon act!

But, know also that it is God's will that all sorts of men should be saved and come to an accurate knowledge of the truth.

Also, would you want your loved ones to follow you and the rest of deceived humanity into destruction at Armageddon, surely not? Why, because you love them and want only the very best for them, which is exactly what God wants for you. Why, because you are part of His human family and because

God is love, He loves us, despite all! But, Justice demands that he act and act He will at Armageddon!

Is history repeating itself? In the run up to the Second World War in Britain much of what we are now experiencing was going on back then. There were the few desperately trying to warn about Hitler's Nazi Germany and where matters were heading, while for the majority it was a case of anything for peace, the cry was "Peace in Our Time." Fortunately, as had happened before in British history during the time of the Spanish Armada, it was the resolute stand taken by Queen Elizabeth l, that preserved the Sovereignty of England and was instrumental in preventing England from becoming part of the Spanish Catholic Empire, thus allowing Britain to go on to become a first rate naval power with an empire upon which the sun would never set and also to establish the thirteen colonies that would become the New England States and the cornerstone upon which the United States was built!

Likewise, it was Churchill who later took a similar position before and during the Second World War only to be booted out of office once the war was over by the very same crowd of deceived individuals who had tried to block him from taking the nation to war. Are things any different this time around? Is it not the same evil forces that are determined as ever to foist the One World government upon us and if they are not challenged, they will surely succeed. At this late stage having infiltrated what remains of the once 'free-world' there is really not much standing in their way. Needless to say that should not provide a reason for you to surrender your God given Sovereigntyι

It is through placemen occupying positions of power in big government, business and religion that the Illuminati agenda is carried out. Yes, Satan's tactics never change, why because they work! It's always about money and power and man's lust for it. (the R-complex at work within us) So it is that these ones that control every aspect of our lives, set the norms and demand blind conformity and the obedience of the human 'herd.' Do not allow yourself to be suckered into following the 'lemming run' over the cliff into oblivion at Armageddon because that is where matters are heading.

The evil is incredible, the mental, emotional and physical onslaught, the manipulation of virtually every aspect of our lives. It's all about control. The finger prints of our unseen controllers are in evidence everywhere. In Medicine, the drug cartels with their intellect suppressing and mind destroying drugs aspartame, Prozac, Ritalin, fluoride dumped into the water supply, immune destroying vaccines, the aids scam, pandemic brain tumors, pseudo heart attacks. Education 2000 – it's iron fisted control of the curriculum, control of science, control of the environment is further evidence of their manipulation. Global 2000, the New American Century....programs designed to destroy the ability for 'critical thinking,' while promoting and encouraging the 'herd' mentality, knowing that like sheep, generally are followers... Also, programs for biological warfare against the population and the food supply.... to stop people being mentally, emotionally and physically healthy, the list goes on.

The Illuminati's control of money translates into their controlling the world. <u>The problems of poverty, debt, war are made to happen because it makes humanity</u>

easier to control. And likely only a huge recession would fix today's broken financial system

'Allow me to issue and control the money of a nation, and I care not who writes the law'.....Mayer Anschel Rothschild.

It has been said that after 9/11 beneath one of the Twin Towers, were tunnels which served as a major terminal between the underground society and the surface society it controls.

Also, underneath most major cities especially in the US are subterranean counterpart cities .Similar facilities exist in many other countries around the world in Central and South America, Britain, Egypt, Mesopotamia, Turkey, Asia, China, Malta and elsewhere. In New Mexico there is the infamous Dulce underground facility or what might better be described as a chamber of horrors. High speed monorail trains connect the systems.

Timothy Good in his book *Unearthly Disclosures* confirms the existence of other extraterrestrial bases. The reliability of these sources was supported by Admiral of the Fleet, Lord Hill-Norton, the former chief of the UK Defense Staff and former chairman of the NATO Military Committee.

 Many bases that are underwater exist in Australia, the Pacific, the former Soviet Union, the USA and the Caribbean. These are permanent alien bases. He also said they were 'messing' with plate tectonics, the movement of land that causes earthquakes, as in Sunami's. Also that the warming of the world's oceans was connected to extraterrestrial activity - it was not global warming that was causing the problem.

In many instances, members of the military above the rank of major are aware of the situation but are sworn to secrecy. Is this the kind of world order you would want to live in?

The white unmarked aircraft seen on many airport runways around the world are there not without a reason! As are the 'Concentration or Detainment Centers and Re-Education Centers, that are rumored to be spread out across America under Rex-84 and also in other countries and parts of the world ? Operation 'Night Train' code name for a nation wide pre-dawn round up of those considered undesirable or unsuitable for the New World Order.

The Fincen Mission, a U.N./U.S. Program for 'House to house search and seizure of property and arms, A 'separation and categorization' of people as prisoners in large numbers, especially those considered as dangerous to 'Law and Order' because they are not ready to collaborate with the implementation of a New World Order. The huge data bases that are said to exist containing every-ones information. Super computers in Brussels and America! All this and only muted silence from....'We the People.'

So, that is the big picture showing what really is going on. This ungodly world is wicked, sick and it's ruler evil, so be resolved in your heart to '**Seek Him Early**' Hosea 5:15.

THE MAYAN CALENDAR

The base resonant frequency of the planet, discovered in 1899 and known as the Schumann Cavity Resonance, remained pretty constant until the mid - 1980s when it began to quicken rapidly...the effect of these higher vibrations is that 'time' appears to be passing much faster. The Maya peoples of Mexico in Yucatan left records of the measurement of time...small, medium and great circles of the Earth's evolution. **One of the great cycles is due to be completed in 2012.** The vibrational frequency of the planet is changing as it completes this vast cycle and enters another. That we are now in the year 2016 again shows that we are far into the 'final part of the days' and also God's patience, kindness and mercy in allowing 'Extra time.'

 Some call the new cycle....the Age of Aquarius as the earth moves through the area of the heavens dubbed 'Pices.' While, researchers, physics and mystics suggest that our frequency is getting closer every day to the fourth - dimensional range.

This will explain why the reptilians are having to work harder to hold human form and thus the urgency for completion of their agenda which is the complete control of the planet and to turn its peoples into mind controlled slaves. The human micro-chip called Digital Angel (Angel-Reptilian) Apple-Digital, is already ahead of schedule. Dr Peter Zhou chief scientist of DigitalAngel.net of course has stressed the benefits of people becoming human robots controlled and connected by satellite, according to him implants will become as popular as cell phones. One of his most chilling statements was that DA will be a connection from yourself to the electronic world...your guardian and protector.

This ties in with what the Mayan Mexican Indians refer to as the 'final baktun' that explains that driven by ego, materialism and money, history and mankind will have reached a kind of saturation point, where history simply will have nowhere to go! So certainly for us it is a matter of faith to know that God's Millennium of Peace is at hand!

Zulu historian, Credo Mutwa in his book *Song of the Stars* provides a similar account of space aliens that the Zulu's call the Mzungu ,the 'Watchers,' reptilian men with lizard like faces, living in the 'kingdom of the shadows, in the 4th dimension outside the human frequency wave bands who are able to enter or exit our dimension or reality at will.

That certain leading politicians, banking and business leaders, media owners, heads of the military and others are serpents in human form. Staggering as this may seem in the minds of people, to most it would be 'utter nonsense.' As Credo Mutwa explains, 'the union between people from the stars and humanity is depicted in virtually every ancient culture and because the situation for humanity is now so perilous it is more important for people to know about this than for him to keep his vows of silence.